Interior: Universiteitsoord Dutch Reformed Church, Pretoria

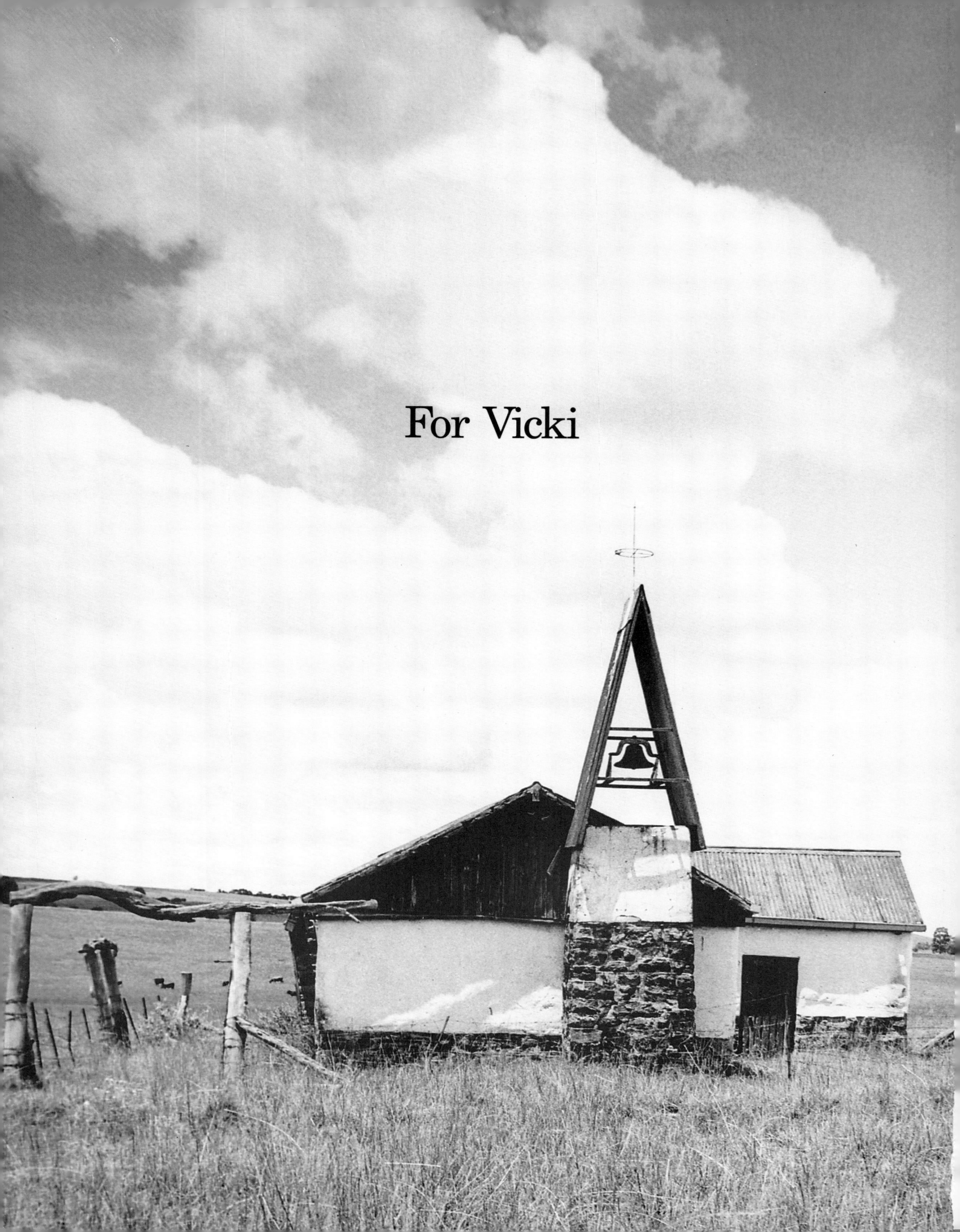

For Vicki

Places of Worship in South Africa

John Oxley

SOUTHERN
BOOK PUBLISHERS

Previous publications by the author

Down Where No Lion Walked

The photograph of old St Georges Cathedral on page 37 is reproduced with permission from the South African Library, Cape Town.

The quotation from *Cry, The Beloved Country* by Alan Paton on page 106 is reproduced with permission of Charles Scribner's Sons, New York, an imprint of Macmillan Publishing Company, and the Random Century Group, London.

The painting of *Nagmaal* on page 156 by Willem Coetzer is reproduced with permission from the Durban Art Gallery and Mr and Miss Coetzer, the heirs of the artist.

The photograph of the swearing-in of Mr F. W. de Klerk as State President (page 166) is reproduced with the permission of the South African Communication Service.

Copyright © 1992 by the author

All rights reserved. No part of this publication may be reproduced or transmitted in any form or by any means without prior written permission from the publisher.

Standard Edition ISBN 1 86812 424 X
Collectors' Edition ISBN 1 86812 443 6
First edition, first impression 1993

Published by
Southern Book Publishers (Pty) Ltd
PO Box 3103, Halfway House, 1685

Photography © by John Oxley for SPIX International

Book design and typography by
Richard Collins, D&R Design cc, Pretoria

Set in 12/14pt and 10/11pt New Century Schoolbook

Reproduction by Remata Bureau and Printers (Pty) Ltd, Midrand

Printed and bound by Creda Press (Pty) Ltd, Cape

Different creeds are but different paths to reach the Almighty.
Various are the ways that lead to the house of the Lord.
Every religion is nothing but one of such paths that lead to God.

Sri Ramakrishna (1836-1886)

" . . . *they will hammer their swords into ploughshares* . . ."

Isaiah 2 : 4

The symbolism implicit in the conversion of weapons of war into instruments of peace, described by Isaiah, may be seen to have a modern parallel in the charming little chapel of St Peter in Chains at the Old Fort in Durban, where the historic powder magazine, surrounded by its heavy protective anti-blast walls, built by the British garrison in the last century, has been made into a peaceful place of worship.

xi Preface

xiii Acknowledgements

1 Before the Coming of the Foreigners

17 The Coming of the Foreigners

Places of Worship

33 Cape Province

91 Natal

131 Transvaal

173 Orange Free State

Cape Province

34 The Groote Kerk
Cape Town

37 The Cathedral Church of
St George the Martyr
Cape Town

40 The Gardens Synagogues
Cape Town

43 Nederduitse Gereformeerde Kerk
Graaff-Reinet

46 The Roman Catholic Mission
Pella

49 The Moffat Mission
Kuruman

52 The Methodist Commemoration Church
Grahamstown

55 The Cathedral of Christ the King
Queenstown

57 The Cathedral of St Michael
and St George
Grahamstown

60 The Holy Trinity Church
Belvidere

63 The Sheikh Yusuf Kramat
Faure

66 The Synagogue
Kimberley

69 The Moravian Mission
Mamre

72 Mission Church of the Holy Cross
Mackay's Nek

75 Nederduitse Gereformeerde Kerk
Cradock

79 The Yellowwood Church of St Andrew
Redbourne

81 The Rhenish Church
Stellenbosch

84 St Patrick on the Hill
Hogsback

86 The Myrtle Rigg Church
Bonnievale

88 St Luke's: A Private Chapel
Onrus

Natal

92 The Church of the Vow
Pietermaritzburg

96 The Roman Catholic Mission
Mariannhill

100 All Saints Church
Ladysmith

103 Griqua National Independent
Church
Kokstad

106 Buddhist Retreat Centre
Ixopo

109 The Yellowwood Chapel of
the Holy Trinity
Bulwer

112 The Soofi Mosque
Ladysmith

115 A Drakensberg Country Church
Cathkin Peak

117 The Shree Poongavana Amman Temple
Durban

119 The Church of the Good Shepherd
Hlabisa

122 The Sri-Sri Radha-Radhanath
Temple of Understanding
Durban

125 The Llandaff Oratory
Van Reenen

127 The Subrahmanya Temple
Tinley Manor

Transvaal

132 **Nederduitsch Hervormde Kerk**
Potchefstroom

135 **The Great Synagogue**
Johannesburg

138 **St Andrew's Presbyterian Church**
Germiston

141 **Nederduitse Gereformeerde Kerk**
Pretoria East

144 **The Zion Christian Church**
Moria

146 **The Greek Orthodox Church**
Pretoria

148 **Nederduitse Gereformeerde Kerk**
Lydenburg

151 **The Mariaman Temple**
Pretoria

154 **Nederduitse Gereformeerde Kerk**
Middelburg

157 **The Lion *Shul***
Johannesburg

159 **The Lutheran Mission**
Botshabelo

162 **The Zionist Church**
Wakkerstroom

164 **Universiteitsoord**
Pretoria

167 **Rhema Church**
Randburg

170 **An Interdenominational Chapel**
Verwoerdburg

Orange Free State

174 **The Tweetoringkerk**
Bloemfontein

178 **St Patrick's Cathedral**
Kroonstad

181 **St Augustine Mission**
Modderpoort

184 **Nederduitse Gereformeerde Kerk**
Winburg

187 **The Berlin Mission**
Bethany

190 **Nederduitse Gereformeerde Kerk**
Senekal

193 **Our Lady of the Assumption**
Qwa Qwa

195 **Nederduitse Gereformeerde Kerk**
Kroonstad

199 Photographic Notes

201 Bibliography

205 Index

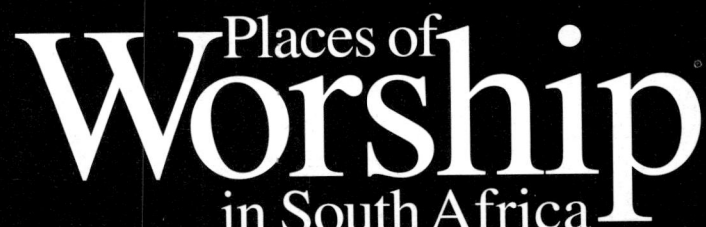

Places of Worship in South Africa

Preface

At the outset let it be accepted that limitations upon the size of this anthology have made it impossible to include more than a relatively few places of worship in its pages. Given the multiplicity of creeds in South Africa and the great number of their places of worship, no single volume could possibly comprehensively encompass a study of such magnitude. The inevitable and understandable constraints have thus made it necessary to select representative examples, the choice of which will surely not result in wholehearted agreement among readers. Such unanimity would be a wild hope rather than a realistic expectation, and the present selection will thus surely be challenged.

We all have our favourite places of worship, though the reasons for those personal choices may not be shared or understood. They may stem perhaps from family tradition — an emotion inherited from childhood. Inevitably, too, there is generally a tendency to favour places we know, places where, for one reason or another, we feel comfortable and at ease. It is hoped that any feelings of disappointment as a result of the omission of a personally favoured place of worship will be compensated for by interest evoked by others included in these pages.

To minimise the inevitability of accusations of personal partiality in the difficult task of winnowing examples for inclusion, certain guidelines were established at the outset and (within the parameters of human judgement) these were observed as far as possible throughout the compilation of a book which aims to please as many readers as possible.

Those guidelines were:

that *different religions and religious opinions* would be represented as broadly as feasible;

that *geographical factors* would be taken into account in these pages — as widely as possible;

that *architecture and architectural features* would (of course) be a major factor in the final choice;

that *historical considerations* would play a role in selection;

that any *unusual factors* concerning an individual place of worship would also be taken into account.

These considerations had to be manifest in the text or the illustrations, or both, so that visual impact inevitably also played a part in the choice of content.

It will be appreciated that these rules were not without conflict among themselves, and they raised a multiplicity of problems in the circumstances of the practical constraints upon space.

Besides searches and researches covering almost three years of specialised reading and discussions, many thousands of kilometres were travelled far and wide throughout South Africa, in the course of which several hundred places of worship were studied *in situ*.

For each place of worship here illustrated, there are numbers of others of equal significance, of equal beauty and interest which circumstances have crowded from these pages.

In so many ways, the subject is a rich one, richer than mere words and photographs can adequately tell, for words and illustrations — however good — lack the warmth and the emotion created by the tangible manifestations of an invisible inner faith and of silent and essentially personal religious beliefs.

No less is the subject a wide one; its breadth and depth go beyond the scope of this anthology. Factors of religion, history and architecture generally tend to vary proportionately with the individual examples which themselves illustrate — and illuminate — the subject as a whole.

Not only do our places of worship in South Africa demonstrate the considerable diversity of faiths in the country, as well as much of their history and ways of life, and the aspirations and arts of their adherents, but these religious shrines also illustrate something of the cultures of the manifold elements in the congealing amalgam of this young, heterogeneous and developing nation.

However tangential still, the increasing contact and association of the various elements of the population in the realms of faith and through those places of worship are a demonstrable response to the country's national credo — *Ex Unitate Vires*. If a study such as this — eschewing didactic aims — happens to enlarge the spectrum of understanding among the diverse components of the population and happens to add some further understanding towards a common destiny, then it will have helped to realise yet more the hopes of those who created those shrines and, too, it will have achieved more indeed than its author expected.

J.O.
Pretoria

Acknowledgements

Understandably, dealing with the wide spectrum of places of worship in South Africa has necessitated considerable research, mainly into religion, history and architecture, the primary components in the philosophies and the fabric of the various individual examples of the subject.

At the same time, however, studies have had also to range more widely than merely across those broad categories, and the mechanics of such research — not least, travel across much of the country — necessarily added further dimensions and ancillary responsibilities to the task.

It would have been impossible to undertake all those responsibilities singlehanded, and the completion of this project has not been without the assistance of many people along the way.

That help has been varied in its nature and has been rendered by a wide spectrum of helpers. It could be said that the only elements common throughout have been their enthusiasm, their faith in the outcome of the project, and the breadth and depth of the personal encouragement which their co-operation brought to bear on the work.

Details of that assistance are too diverse conveniently to be listed here. At the same time, the extent of any list of the names of helpers makes its inclusion similarly not really feasible — not least, too, for fear of any hapless, inadvertent omissions.

It is not the size of a single piece which is important in the completion of any jigsaw puzzle. In that sense, the smallest piece is as vital and as important as any one of the others. So it has been with the compilation of this book: the help received cannot be individually quantified.

For the word-of-mouth advice about unusual places of worship in South Africa I am grateful to many friends. For assistance in garnering details about those shrines, I thank numbers of church officials throughout the country — clergy as well as laity, secretaries and scribas, archivists and historians. Numbers of architects have generously given time, information and advice and I thank them too for their co-operation, as also do I thank academics of various disciplines who have suggested useful references. Librarians have pointed the way to source material, while the National Monument Councils in the various provinces have responded helpfully to enquiries and queries. To all these and especially to supportive friends I am most grateful.

But, above all — and not as a duty only — I thank Vicki, my wife, to whom this book is dedicated, for her infinite co-operation, encouragement and her help in endless ways during the several years I have been bonded to this task.

Before the Coming of the Foreigners

outh Africa is a young country on an old continent. It yet has no places of worship to compare in age with the historic temples and magnificent cathedrals of many other lands whose cultures reach through centuries and millennia deep into misty antiquity.

The fascination of any study of places of worship in South Africa lies not in the age of their fabric. For them history is in the making and the patina of age has still to gild and ennoble them.

Interest here lies instead in the rich variation of cultures and religions which have come to a young country that, historically, lies between east and west and where the meeting of the two provided not only impetus to an age of accelerating progress everywhere, but also for the creation of a rich mosaic of religions and cultures of its own. It is not antiquity alone which embellishes a culture with interest, however.

To make comparisons on the basis of age between such places of worship as South Africa possesses and those of older civilisations is a temptation which must be resisted, for South Africa has nothing comparable to offer. Demands inherent in the opening up of a raw land and in coming to terms with other cultures and conditions in many ways has deprived the settlers of time in which to create a style and an art of their own. In assessing aspects of its recent and contemporary culture, South African society should be seen as being younger than its years.

Places of worship in this land must be seen in a context of their own. The young nation is a crucible in which a bubbling mixture of diverse races and people is fusing into a unique amalgam that eventually will take on cultural characteristics of its own, characteristics that, with the patina of its own history, will reveal its own individual beauty. But that fusion has yet to come. The amalgam has yet to blend and to cool. In the meantime, its people, energies directed at subsistence development, live with the cultures — the changing cultures — of their respective pasts.

While Africa is the oldest of all the world's continents and, as the cradle of man himself, has thus been inhabited by humans for longer than anywhere else, modern Africa is not heir to the rich historical legacies of earlier inhabitants in the manner that numbers of other lands and societies have been blessed.

The descendants of early man — in the place where man evolved — have marked their passing tenancy with their bones alone, while later generations have left no permanent examples of their evolving skills and civilisations. Historically their lives were as ephemeral and as intangible as the winds of the changing seasons. Such evidence as early man did leave behind was left unconsciously and as unwittingly as the print of a passing foot in powdered sand. Those were antique traces of his animal being — bones left to be fossilised in limestone and rock — but relics of his evolving skills are limited to his subsistence.

Although geologically Africa is the oldest of the world's continents, in a historical sense it should perhaps be regarded as a modern phenomenon. Until recently, little was known either of its past or of those who peopled the land. In recent millennia there seemed to be no inducements to probe that darkness, and a blanket of ignorance continued to conceal what the "dark continent" contained and what its indigenous people were like. Only relatively recently has the enveloping mantle of mystery and ignorance begun to be lifted.

There are indications that traders from India had contact with the African littoral as long ago as the fifteenth century BC. A surviving petroglyph, which once decorated an Egyptian temple, shows slaves being loaded aboard a galley of Queen Hatshepsut's fleet at Punt, now thought perhaps to be on the coast of East Africa.

The Phoenician circumnavigation of Africa six centuries before the birth of Christ led to no rush to explore its interior. The people of Europe and the Middle East, whose civilisations dominated those centuries, showed no enthusiasm to venture into a land contiguous and near at hand, yet long before the advent of Christianity they had developed links across the vastness of Asia, creating a highway which reached to the other side of the world.

Not even the ancient Egyptians who built the mighty pyramids and the fascinating sphinx were tempted to expand their dominions southward into the heart of Africa.

In the fifth century BC, however, Carthage attempted to extend its trading beyond the confines of the Mediterranean by establishing colonies on the west coast of Africa.

By any standards it was a massive movement of people. It is said that in some 60 ships 30 000 men and women were transported to be set ashore at various points along the coast to establish settlements at sites as far south as the southwestern corner of the continent's bulge — near what is now Sierra Leone — and to create colonies for the development of friendly relations with the indigenous people of the area.

Those settlements endured for some years before dying out. During their lifetime no effort seems to have been made to penetrate further inland, however, and for several centuries the interior continued to exist as a closed book, though Roman expeditions probed southward from the Mediterranean into the Sahara desert.

Records remain scanty and it was left to modern scientists to unlock Africa's ancient archives. In doing so, they uncovered the mystery of man's origins and revealed evidence of man's history from his beginnings, more than two-million years ago, and to document his physical evolution and his early existence on the world's oldest continent.

The first hint about man's origins came with Charles Darwin's startling speculation in 1871 that "... it is somewhat more probable that our early progenitors lived on the African continent than elsewhere..." This thesis in turn had to wait more than half a century for any sort of confirmation.

It came from South Africa with Professor Raymond Dart's discovery in 1923 of a fossilised skull at Taung in the north of the Cape Province which turned the scientific spotlight on the beginnings of man and provided the confirmation which archaeological speculation needed. Dart's claims did not go unchallenged, however. His theories that the fossil derived from early man himself and was the "missing link" between ape and human brought abuse from many quarters of the scientific world — understandably cautious after the embarrassment of the hoax of the so-called Piltdown Man. Robert Broom's discovery of a similar skull in the limestone deposits of a cave at Sterkfontein in the Transvaal caused hostile opinion to subside and led scientists to accept that Africa was indeed the cradle of mankind. The belief hardened into scientific fact with further discoveries and researches in East Africa.

Africa would thus seem to have been a close witness to the full range of man's development. No longer is that disputed. Nowhere else has man existed for so long. It was from Africa that early man migrated, first about 1,5 million years ago, to other places where he continued to evolve and develop.

The fashioning of the first simple tools, developed from pebbles during the Lower Palaeolithic age, was probably African man's finest contribution to human development: "A big step for man, a leap for mankind." By definition it was that which distinguished ape from man; triggering a whole new mode of living and culture. The significance of that evolutionary development cannot be overrated.

But from then on the development of man in Africa seems to have proceeded more slowly than that of those who had migrated from the continent and settled elsewhere. In Africa man remained a simple nomadic hunter-gatherer while human lifestyles were changing radically elsewhere. It was not until about 10 000 years ago that waves of people sweeping into Africa from the Middle East introduced new ways of living. With them they brought a knowledge of agriculture — the tilling of fields, the planting and reaping of crops. It was a wholly new way of life; a settled rather than a nomadic style of living: the start of a fresh era.

But for all that added knowledge and their developing skills, neither they nor their descendants appear to have contributed to the continent's history lasting monuments of their passing existence — apart from their bones. With one exception, no enduring memorials mark their tenancy of the areas they once inhabited, nor shrines to whatever deities they may have revered. Through the ages there have been no written records. The telling of Africa's story has been left to others — to aliens.

Nowhere across the length and breadth of the continent have there been found, for example, huge ziggurats such as the ancient Sumerians built more than 4 000 years ago, nor in Africa have there been uncovered remains of indigenous stone temples and magnificently constructed and decorated halls, such as the Persians left to posterity a millennium ago.

Nowhere on the vast grassy plains of the continent where African men lived and hunted is there evidence that these early people created religious temples, such as circles of rough hewn megaliths to catch the first dawning daylight of summer solstices as the ancient Britons did at Stonehenge; monuments scientifically planned and raised 2 500 years ago.

The world's oldest continent and its first men offer no historical African Troy, no rich Mycenae for some latter-day Schliemann to uncover.

The northern regions of Africa possess the continent's oldest monuments, the vast pyramids in Egypt built by another civilisation more than 2 500 years before the Christian era began.

Through the long era of his existence, African man would seem to have created nothing to match the glory and splendour of Greek or Roman architectural monuments built millennia ago. No desert in Africa has yielded other relics of "vast and trunkless legs of stone" created by indigenous people. Nor have its jungles, in obliterating scars left by nomadic man's habitation, preserved for posterity any vast and ornate temples to match man's magnificent creations in Cambodia. Nothing of indigenous origin has been uncovered in Africa to equal the splendour of ancient Mayan architecture and art in central America on the other side of the world. Along all the lengthy coasts of Africa, no giant sculptured heads brave strong salt-laden winds and the rain as, with deep set unblinking eyes, they gaze watchfully out to sea as do those granite monuments left by Polynesians on Easter Island in the broad Pacific.

In Africa, man has left remarkably little evidence of his long sojourn here. Relative to those ages, traces of his endeavours are sparse indeed, while evidence of a developing culture comes hard to hand. But, when all is said and done, being nature's own greatest achievement, man himself remains the world's most spectacular creation, Africa's finest monument. As Professor Revil Mason of the University of the Witwatersrand avers, the golden helmets, the marble gods and the sumptuous temples of the world's civilisations all "came later, after the hard work of becoming human had been done."

African man was essentially a primitive hunter-gatherer whose nomadic existence in a vast open land was the antithesis of any settled living that would induce him to create lasting buildings and monuments. The development of agriculture — necessitating settled living — which spilled into Africa from the Middle East did little to change African man's style of living. He merely moved on, into the reaches of the continent, avoiding change and seemingly untouched by such intruding influences; those with animals taking their cattle with them.

He has, however, bequeathed to history some evidence of his recent cultural past in Africa, examples exceptional enough in an otherwise uniquely historical vacuum to lead to speculation, to controversy and doubt regarding their origins and authorship.

The most significant of the exceptions is, of course, Great Zimbabwe, an impressive mass of carefully crafted stone buildings sprawling over more than seven square kilometres. Situated in the midst of what was an ancient gold entrepôt centre, the complex was in a ruined state when first seen by European explorers towards the end of the fifteenth century. If these ruins were indeed built unaided by Africans, then, without doubt, these stone buildings remain the most important extant historical achievement of African man, albeit — according to scientific dating — relatively modern.

It was long argued, however, that the construction of these buildings would seem to be beyond the innate skill of the early people of the region. Africans do not build in stone, which has led to the conclusion that these buildings were therefore the work of peoples from elsewhere — migrants from Yemen perhaps in biblical times; or, perhaps, peoples from India. Certainly the centre had been known to foreign traders for many centuries, as antique objects, found among the ruins, originated from lands as far away as Persia and China. But modern research has demonstrated beyond reasonable doubt that its construction was indeed the work of Africans who, it seems, laboured for many centuries to complete the various buildings — probably, it is thought, from the tenth century onwards. If this estimate is accurate, Zimbabwe is contemporary with the Tower of London and other great buildings of Norman architecture in Europe.

While Great Zimbabwe was clearly an important entrepôt centre and the gold, there refined, was probably its most important trading commodity, it is also believed to have been a religious centre of some significance, though such evidence remains obscure.

The Phoenicians circumnavigated Africa and in later years there was contact with Africa both from the north-east and the north-west long before ships linked Europe and southern Africa and the Portuguese had roughly mapped Africa's southern coastline. Even then, however, for two further centuries the interior of the continent remained untouched and unknown to Europeans.

With increasing frequency in the decades after their ships began sailing into the Indian Ocean, the Portuguese and

Dutch navigators made contact with the Khoikhoi (Hottentots), bartering goods for meat when their ships put into Table Bay for fresh water and food. Sporadic contact became permanent when, in 1652, the Dutch established a permanent victualling station at this halfway point on the long voyage from Holland to the East.

While historians differ about the dates when the Khoikhoi first reached southern Africa, it would seem as if, with their cattle, they had migrated into the region probably between 4 000 and 2 000 years before the coming of those first European settlers. In stages they came from the north and their language indicated they were peoples who had earlier had contact with the inhabitants of the Sudan. They also knew how to smelt copper and were able to work iron, which they used to reinforce the sharp tips of their spears and arrows.

In their long, slow march down the eastern side of Africa, and during their sojourn in these southern regions, the Khoikhoi had created no buildings to mark the progress either of their extended trek or their life at the Cape. They too built neither dwellings that would endure, nor lasting shrines where they might have worshipped whatever spirits and gods existed in their pantheon.

The absence throughout early history of relics of places of worship is not to be seen, however, as an indication that these indigenous people were without religious beliefs.

The multiplicity of tribes throughout the continent led, inevitably, to a broad assortment of varying customs and beliefs. There were no substantial universal religions, no formalised systems of belief common to them all. Those came later — much later — with the advent of Christianity and of the Moslem religion. Within each historic community, however, established beliefs and customs governed social conduct and daily living and which, however pagan by later standards, tended to be governed by an acceptance of an invisible mystical higher authority who, all seeing, would mete out punishment to miscreants and any who breached the accepted social norms and tribal mores.

For those early people religion was essentially an element of life, rather than a distinctly separate activity which might or might not be practised as one wished. Religion was inherent in living, a simple and unconscious faith in the nature of life itself.

But while aspects of these beliefs in Africa certainly differed from community to community, a common thread ran through them all. Nature, the universal provider, was worshipped. And, too, there was generally a common acceptance of a Supreme Being who had created the world and given life and who governed man's destiny, both collectively and individually. Belief in life after death was widespread and it was generally held that the deceased returned to earth in spirit form to be agents of the Supreme Being, and who, as his representatives, might be consulted when advice and help from higher authority were required.

Early European writings about the Khoikhoi reveal differing opinions regarding the religious customs of these indigenous people whom those first Dutch settlers encountered at the Cape. An early writer, indeed, has asserted that the Hottentots "... were devoid of all religious observance except for a custom they have in moonshiny nights of dancing in the fields, of which if you ask 'em the reason all their answer is that it is a custom of the Hottentots, and was so of their forefathers..."

If judged by European norms, the assertion that the Hottentots had no religion at all would perhaps be difficult to refute. Possibly confusion arose from the breadth of difference between the inherently formalised and established European beliefs, on the one hand, and, on the other, the Hottentot system of deifying and worshipping natural forces and phenomena of nature. Later research has revealed that these negroid peoples certainly possessed well-established beliefs and practices of their own and that superstitions exercised powerful influence — akin to religion — upon them and on their daily lives. For them, too, good and evil were basic concepts in their religion.

The main heroes in the Hottentot pantheon were Tsui-Goab and Heitsi Eibib, both personifications of benevolent forces, men of great physical strength and hunting skills, possessing considerable supernatural powers, while Gaunab, on the other hand, was a prominent mythical chief imbued with the forces of evil and associated with dark spirits and death.

But while it was largely the Hottentots with whom those early European settlers initially came into contact, they were not the first indigenous peoples to inhabit the region. Some thousands of years before the migrating Hottentots arrived there, the hunter-gatherer San (Bushman) already inhabited parts of southern Africa. At the time of the arrival of the Dutch, however, San settlements were inland, away from Table Bay and the coast, and it was not until three years after their arrival that the European settlers, exploring inland, first encountered these people.

They were tiny, incredibly nimble, and slit-eyed, often with a fold of skin attached to the eyelid, a characteristic of Mongoloid people. Their hair grew in short tufts. Though much smaller in stature than the Hottentots, with whom they share common ancestral origins, the nomadic Bushmen are lighter-skinned than either the Khoikhoi or the Bantu and are generally characterised — especially the women — by unusually prominently protruding buttocks. Certain physical characteristics common to the San and to the ancient Egyptians, together with a Mongoloid touch to the eyes, strengthened later theories that these people were descendants of migrants who, long before, had wandered southwards from those far northern regions of Africa.

In Namibia recent radiocarbon datings of objects in caves, where occupation by ancient Bushmen was marked by their remarkable paintings on the rock walls, revealed that some of the works of art were probably done about 26 000 years ago, making them by far the oldest known works of art in all Africa and, too, several thousand years older than the earliest examples of rock art yet uncovered in Europe. While evidence indicates that these works of art in Namibia were probably executed by ancient Bushmen, authoritative scientific confirmation is still not forthcoming. Other such works, generally referred to as "Bushman paintings", are reckoned to be of later origin, having been executed within the past 6 000 years.

Though without a working knowledge of metals, such as the Hottentots had, the Bushman has given the world his unique brand of painting, discovering and developing pigments to decorate the rocky walls of his cave dwellings where he has lived. They are among the finest examples of primitive art known to the world.

But though in recent millennia the Bushman had technical knowledge enough to create his own pigments and the Hottentot had rudimentary skills which enabled him to smelt copper and iron, neither peoples knew how to work clay to make bricks or pottery containers, nor did they know how to cut and bind rocks and stone with which to create buildings.

Their usual dwellings, simply fashioned, were suited to their nomadic habits and the prevailing climatic requirements: simple light frames, made by bending cut saplings and covered with reed mats, all conveniently portable. The organic nature of the materials precluded preservation for posterity. Fortunately nature provided enduring shelter — caves — where the Bushman was able to leave his art for the admiration of later generations.

While that art has not the monumental magnificence of the pyramids, nor the sophisticated beauty of any ancient Greek temple, nor the rich splendour of Aztec gold ornaments, the significance of those rock paintings lies in their uniqueness and in the secrets they hold.

Much of their value lies in the evidence which this early art provides for historians. Brilliantly these pictures relate the fables of their people, depict the activities of their days and, for the future, have left valuable traces of their unique culture.

The Bushman artist's use of simple monochromatic and bichromatic forms, together with his technique in the handling of shading and modelling in his paintings, was followed by a demonstrable ability to use techniques of foreshortening and perspective to a degree rare and unusual — if not unique — in primitive art.

Today only a handful of Bushmen remain. The fact that they now live mostly in the Kalahari has given rise to the idea that they are inherently desert folk. But that is not so. In recent millennia they once inhabited the greater part of southern Africa, occupying fertile regions as far north as Sofala in East Africa — where, as recently as a thousand years ago, they were known to eastern travellers as the Wak-Wak people — and even leaving their skeletal remains as far north as Egypt, in regions where, in ages long before, they probably originated.

The Bushmen lived generally in small communal groups, seldom more than a hundred persons in each, but usually far fewer. As hunter-gatherers they moved on when an area was cleared of the staple edible herbs and roots and when the numbers of the animals in the region were reduced by the bows and poisoned arrows of these wily little hunters.

In bountiful times the land provided abundant room for all. There was adequate space in which to move, vast tracts of fresh country in which to live. But by the mid-seventeenth century, for the Bushmen especially, the sands of those halcyon days began running out.

New peoples were moving into the region; from the north migrating blacks with their cattle, and from the south a small group of white-skinned people who came from the sea, stepping from the backs, it seemed, of large sea-birds with large white wings. Ashore they at once began constructing buildings of solid materials of a sort and size the nomadic Bushmen and Hottentots had not dreamed of.

It is not clear when the first southward-migrating Bantu penetrated the tsetse-fly belt across the north-eastern side of southern Africa, that formidable barrier which threatened humans and their beasts with dreaded "sleeping sickness" that brings death to those infected. Perhaps it was this natural cordon which controlled the numbers entering south Africa from the north, limiting early migration.

But eventually, probably by the third century AD, enough people had breached the cordon to develop settlements in the fertile regions of the country lying between the Drakensberg and the ocean. These grew in number through the centuries, expanding to take up more and more of the available land. In the ensuing competition for space, it was inevitable that the Bantu should clash with the resident Bushmen of the region, clashes that were exacerbated by the Bushmen's pilfering of the Bantu's livestock — which the little hunters regarded merely as prey to be hunted in the same way as they had always freely hunted whatever wild game came to hand within their established territory.

While contending with these invaders on a northern front, as it were, the Bushmen faced the European settlers spreading outwards and inland from the shores of Table Bay. In doing so, the white settlers, ignorant of the territorial conventions, invited retaliation by encroaching upon the established hunting grounds of the indigenous inhabitants.

The history of this developing hostility is not a record to be proud of. The Bushman, regarded as a thief and a nuisance, was hunted by both black and white spreading further and further across the country, eventually themselves to clash in the competition for land. In the process the Bushman, his numbers greatly reduced, was driven into remoter areas.

While the progenitors of South Africa's Bantu may well have had a hand in the building of the Great Zimbabwe complex and certainly knew how to smelt and work iron, as well as possessing considerable skill in crafting pottery, the various tribes which proliferated south of the Limpopo from the main groups of migrants have contributed nothing similar of substantial architectural or constructional significance in this more southerly region: only in recent centuries a few — very few — scattered groups of corbelled stone huts and, in the grassy centre areas of the Transvaal, the erection of some simple low stone walls, presumably for the purpose of coralling and protecting cattle. Their dwellings were generally circular beehive-shaped huts, clustered into family and tribal groups, fashioned from dried thatching grass, sometimes with low walls of mud and dung supporting the roofs.

Abandoned when the occupants moved on, these dwellings were soon destroyed by the elements. Inexorably nature healed the scars; by degrees vegetation won back the once-trampled earth where kraals and fields had been, and traces of human occupation soon were wiped from sight.

It is improbable indeed in such circumstances that any great everlasting relics were left for later generations of archaeologists. Certainly none has been discovered or unearthed. At best small objects — discarded — may have been inadvertently left behind and absorbed into the freshly developing strata of the continually evolving earth, their future significance perhaps to be exaggerated for researchers by the very paucity of these remains.

Whereas the religion of the San and the Khoikhoi centred upon the worship of nature, the religious philosophy of the Bantu focused upon worship of ancestral spirits. True, the Bantu also accepted the existence of a Creator. He was a mystical Being who had created mankind in a bed of reeds, but, it has been suggested, in the pantheon of religious mythology that was merely a convenient explanation of man's beginnings. That accepted, this Creator plays no further role of any significance in the traditional system of Bantu beliefs.

For these people, their religions required no shrines. No places of worship were constructed; no lasting religious memorials have been found.

Magic and the force of ancestral spirits, on the other hand, were all-important in their life and living, the spirits demanding constant attention and making their presence felt to their descendants in a multitude of ways. Traditionally these spirits took many forms; at times appearing in the form of animals, sometimes as plants and frequently as reptiles, especially snakes, indicating a need for some propitiation of the spirits. Tributes, in the form of ritual killing of cattle, were paid to the spirits at harvest time and at the death of tribal elders and chiefs.

Interestingly, in drawing parallels between certain original beliefs of the pagan Bantu and those of Christianity, recent writers have suggested that these Africans draw a distinction between the death of a man and that of a beast. When it dies, an animal is simply "dead": but for humans death means that the deceased has merely left this earth but retains his soul in another place. This concept would seem to be bound up with the idea of ancestor worship, for if ancestral spirits are to continue to supervise the well-being of their families, then the spirit cannot die but must continue its existence.

The concept of a peaceful afterlife would thus seem — coincidentally — to be common to both Bantu and Christian. But many years were to pass after the arrival of the Europeans before the communion of these common beliefs became extended in the gradual acceptance by the Bantu and other African peoples of formalised religion — based largely, but not solely, on the Christian beliefs of the dominant group of newcomers to southern Africa.

This flowering of religion throughout Africa in the late twentieth century came at a time when the influence of the Christian church in the northern hemisphere seemed to be ebbing. In Africa it is being accompanied by a booming interest in ecclesiastical art unmatched since the splendour of the European Renaissance, developing a powerful ethnic individuality which, shaking off the slumbers of millennia, would seem suddenly to reflect the existence and emergence of a vibrant African character.

The Coming of the Foreigners

The often-held idea of Africa as a continent of heathens tends to overshadow the historical facts that Judaism came to Ethiopia in the tenth century BC and that Christianity first reached there more than a hundred years before it arrived in England. Christianity came directly from where it began — not far away — brought by the Copts down the Red Sea, and the country itself was converted to Christianity by a missionary from Tyre as early as the fourth century. For many long centuries these faiths remained limited to this north-eastern region of the continent, however.

When Christianity did reach South Africa — more than a thousand years later — it came from a wholly different direction. Blocked by the deserts and other geographical obstacles, southern Africa had no contact with the Middle East, and Christianity came to South Africa via Europe, slowly and across vast oceans which at that time were unexplored and seldom traversed — unlike the Christianity that came to Ethiopia, early and quickly along trade routes, ancient and already well established.

Only in the middle of the seventeenth century, when the Dutch East India Company, trading between Europe and the East, had established a refreshment station on the shores of Table Bay, did the Christian faith begin to have a base in the southern regions of the continent.

From that coastal base at the southern tip of the continent Christianity grew and spread, being joined by other faiths along its crusading way.

While looking at various places of worship created by these faiths in modern South Africa, it may be helpful to know something of the general background which led to their creation. Inevitably those developments are woven into the fabric of the nation's history.

Understandably, constraints upon the length and the detail of that background make any discourse necessarily brief.

Prior to the founding of that base at the Cape and following the discovery of a sea route from Europe to the East, attempts had been made to plant the seeds of Christianity at more northerly points along the Indian Ocean coast. Sporadic sparks of Christianity had flared along parts of Africa's east coast. But these died out — were snuffed out — before they could provide any semblance of a link between the existence of the faith in Ethiopia and the southern parts of the continent.

It was commerce rather than any conscious crusading zeal, however, which led to the advent of Christianity in east and southern Africa. The severance of the Silk Road in the mid-fifteenth century had led Europe to seek alternative links with the East and the Portuguese took the lead in that search. Their navigators opened up a route which led their ships around the southern tip of Africa.

Religion followed in the footsteps of commerce — missionaries not far behind the merchants — a pattern also followed elsewhere in Africa.

While the Portuguese managed to oust Arab traders from some points on Africa's east coast and, seeking gold, there established posts of their own, the endeavours of the early Portuguese Jesuit missionaries yielded little positive profit in their efforts to win souls. Though the high hopes of those missionaries who arrived in Inhambane in 1560 were not realised, a Christian mission to the African potentate Monomotapa had a flash of success when the ruler agreed to be baptised with some of his tribe.

But there is more to religion than a mere change of faith. Christian practices implied a whole set of fresh values developed by a culture wholly alien to the customs and beliefs of the African. Approached by Father Gonzalo da Silveira, the Monomotapa certainly agreed to the formality of his baptism, but had little intention of affecting changes in his tribal habits and ways of life that clashed head-on with the demands of the religion he had newly assumed. It was unthinkable, for example, that a chief should have only one wife — as Christianity demanded.

Christianity rested lightly on the Monomotapa's shoulders and it was not difficult for Moslem traders, active enemies of Christianity and jealous of the Jesuits' influence, to persuade him to abandon his new-found faith. Commerce had an ally in religious zeal.

Moslems strangled Father Gonzalo da Silveira and threw his body into the river. His death in the cause of religion made him a Christian martyr, the first in south-east Africa.

Missionary endeavours were not deterred by this set-back, however. The Jesuits were followed by the Dominicans, who in 1577 established a mission at Mozambique, further south, where they came face to face with the savagery of the migrating Bantu. Their efforts on behalf of the church, though spread over a longer period, were hardly more successful.

By then the Portuguese had been superseded by the Dutch in the larger field of maritime commerce and it was the growth of trade which led the prosperous Dutch East India Company, in 1652, to send Jan van Riebeeck to set up a station at the Cape of Good Hope to victual its ships on the long voyage from Holland to India.

To what extent the Company initially saw this "depot of provisions for ships" as a permanent settlement remains a matter of some debate.

While in recommendations for the establishment of the refreshment station it had been pointed out that it would serve also to bring many aborigines "to the Christian reformed religion and to God", the personnel of Jan van Riebeeck's party did not include a pastor. Moreover, some 13 years were to elapse before a minister was appointed to the Cape. In the meanwhile, the resident "Sick-comforter" was responsible for both the bodily and spiritual welfare of the officials. His authority was severely limited, however; the scope of his religious functions being defined in terms of his licence issued by the presbytery of Amsterdam. For its religious services the settlement was dependent upon chaplains from passing ships.

Thus it was — as Van Riebeeck's diary records — some five weeks after landfall at Table Bay on 6 April before the first celebration of the Lord's Supper took place at the Cape when a minister from a passing ship became available, though, as the diary earlier tells, there was a "Sunday service" on 14 April aboard one of the ships — after which "we went with all the boats to the Salt River to fish. . . "

To administer the fledgling settlement, Van Riebeeck at once set up a Council of Policy that consisted of himself and the captains of the three ships which had brought the officials and their families to the Cape. The proceedings of the Council's first meeting were opened with a prayer, saying:

> *Since Thou has called us to conduct the affairs of the East India Company here at the Cape of Good Hope and we are now assembled that we may arrive at such decisions as shall be of most service to the Company, and shall conduce to the maintenance of justice, and the propagation and extension (if that*

be possible) of Thy true Reformed Christian Religion among these wild and brutal men, to the praise and glory of Thy name, we pray Thee, O most merciful Father, that Thou wouldest so enlighten our hearts with Thy fatherly wisdom, that all passions, all misconceptions and all similar defects, may be warded from us, and that we may neither purpose nor decide ought but that which shall tend to magnify Thy most holy Name.

The prayer was recorded in the minutes and was used at the commencement of subsequent meetings of the Council.

Notwithstanding the strength of Roman Catholicism in The Netherlands in the first half of the seventeenth century, the growing force of Calvinism had to be reckoned with. A little more than a year prior to Van Riebeeck's arrival at the Cape, the States General of The Netherlands formally resolved to "maintain the true Christian Reformed religion", which in effect made Protestantism the national religion.

Against this background, it was only to be expected that the religion brought to the Cape by the Dutch East India Company should be sternly Protestant. Indeed, during the Company's rule of almost a century and a half, non-Protestants were denied the right to settle at the Cape, a rule abrogated only during the administration of Janssens and De Mist whose decision was upheld by the British when they took over the Cape in 1806.

In Europe the situation made The Netherlands a haven for Protestants fleeing from religious persecution in France, a state of affairs which was exacerbated by Louis XIV's revocation of the Edict of Nantes in 1685. In the circumstances numbers of French — the Huguenots — preferring the uncertainty of a new land to that of an established but intolerant Europe, chose to seek new lives at the Cape, bringing with them ideas and customs that were to add richly to the infant community there and to influence the development of South Africa.

The absence of a cleric in Van Riebeeck's party strengthens the contention that the Dutch East India Company initially had no intention of establishing a permanent settlement at the Cape. Its role lay in commerce: colonisation was the responsibility of government. Whatever the Company may have intended, however, it was not long before unforeseen circumstances compelled change. On expiry of their initial contracts, numbers of officials opted to remain at the Cape as "Free Burgers", and to serve the needs of the small community and, of course, at the same time also of those in the Company's employ, an ordained minister was sent to the Cape.

Historians thus date the formation of South Africa's first church congregation from the arrival of that minister, Johan van Arckel, in 1665. The community church was situated within the Castle, but as the Castle was then being rebuilt, a wooden church was erected within its walls as a temporary place of worship.

The passing years saw increasing numbers of settlers arriving at the Cape and the consequent occupation of areas beyond the immediate vicinity of the Castle. First of the new settlements was the village of Stellenbosch, founded in 1679. Communities required places of worship and the building of churches followed: at Stellenbosch in 1687; at Drakenstein in 1691; Roodezand (now Tulbagh) in 1743; Zwartland (now Malmesbury) in July 1745 and Graaff-Reinet in October 1792. In Cape Town itself, after years of opposition from the Company, the resident Lutherans were permitted to build their own church there in 1780.

Among the servants brought initially to the Cape were a number of Asians — whether Hindu or Moslem records do not relate. The importation of slaves from Malaya added further to the jigsaw of nationalities and religions arriving in South Africa early in its development. Retaining their allegiance to Mecca, these Moslems added richly to the nation's culture and, with numbers of mosques, also to its ecclesiastical architecture.

Today their descendants and other Moslem migrants, numbering about a quarter of a million and living mostly in and around Cape Town, are a colourful community.

Despite the official ban on the practice of non-Protestant faiths in those early years at the Cape, the existence of a number of Roman Catholic residents discreetly revealed itself when a party of Jesuit priests was permitted to come ashore from a passing ship. They were clandestinely visited by numbers of the settlers — Roman Catholics — who availed themselves of the opportunity of making Confessions, though the visiting priests were not permitted to say Mass.

It was not until freedom of worship was officially recognised at the Cape in 1804 that the first Catholic priests arrived and were formally granted the use of a room in the Castle to serve as a chapel.

Despite this delay in any formal acceptance of Catholicism, the Roman Catholics can claim that the first church in South Africa was theirs. Not only was it a Catholic, Bartolomeu Dias, who first erected a cross in South Africa — in 1486 at Algoa Bay — but it was another, Vasco da Gama, who first celebrated Mass on the southern shores of Africa. In 1497 he held a church service at Mossel Bay. Three years later, Joas da Nova built a small chapel there and that was the first place of Christian worship in South Africa.

By then, in Ethiopia and Egypt at the other end of the continent Christianity had been practised for over a thousand years.

Almost 130 years after Da Nova built that little chapel and before the Dutch East India Company's establishment of a revictualling station at the Cape, another place of Christian worship was built in southern Africa — at Plettenberg Bay by the crew of a ship wrecked there. Those who managed to get ashore spent some months constructing two boats from the wreckage of their ship and, with other material from the wreck, also built a small church to serve their spiritual needs during their enforced sojourn on that shore. That place of worship pre-dated Jan van Riebeeck's arrival by more than 20 years.

During the administration by the Dutch East India Company and several decades before the British occupation, Church of England services had been held in Cape Town. As early as 1749, for example, the commodore of a passing British fleet resting in Table Bay sought permission for the naval chaplain to use the Dutch church for a service for Englishmen ashore. Permission was readily granted, and in the years that followed not only were several further such services held there but, with the agreement of the Dutch authorities, a number of British officers were also buried in that church.

It was not until the second British occupation of the Cape in 1806, however, that services were held regularly by the Church of England, and for the following 27 years these were conducted in the Dutch Reformed Church.

Clearly that situation could not endure, and with the importance of the Church of England at the Cape increased after the British occupation and its role further expanded by the waves of English migrants, the first Church of England

Bishopric was established in 1847, when the dynamic Robert Gray became the first Bishop of Cape Town. This was followed a few years later by the appointment of Colenso and Armstrong as Bishops of Natal and the Eastern Cape respectively.

With the 1820 settlers, predominantly Methodist, were a number of Baptists who established churches of their own, first at Salem and then at Grahamstown. Through the years their numbers have grown and the Baptists have been prominent in promoting Christianity among the blacks of South Africa.

Difficulties experienced by the Dutch church in recruiting ministers from Holland were exacerbated by the proliferation of congregations as settlers spread out from Table Bay and as the list of congregations needing pastors lengthened. For help the Dutch Church turned to Scotland where ecclesiastical thinking was closer to their own outlook than elsewhere. Scots ministers, such as Andrew Murray, who answered the call made a significant contribution to the Church's development in South Africa.

Though Jews were living at the Cape prior to the abolition of the law forbidding non-Protestants to settle there, it was not until after 1804 that they were formally permitted to practise their faith and, with the growth in their numbers, the first Hebrew congregation in South Africa was established in 1841 and the first Synagogue was built in 1863. The community was still not a large one, however, and consisted mainly of migrants of German and Dutch origin, together with a handful of Britons who had come to South Africa with the 1820 settlers. With the discovery of diamonds at Kimberley in 1869 the number of Jews in South Africa swelled rapidly, however, and grew further when gold was discovered on the Witwatersrand in 1886, many of them refugees from the pogroms of eastern Europe.

The cultural mosaic being created by the immigration to South Africa of peoples of varying religions and nationalities at that time developed yet further in 1860 when, with shiploads of Indian labourers brought to Natal to work in the sugar cane fields, more Asiatics were added to the pattern. This form of agriculture required a type of labour for which the indigenous Zulus proved to be unsuitable.

Mostly Hindus from southern India, but with about one in five a Moslem, they came on fixed contracts with the guarantee of repatriation at the conclusion of the labour agreement. But when, after five years, their contracts expired, many opted to remain in South Africa — as Dutch East India Company officials had done 200 years earlier — and acquired land of their own on which to settle. In due course, they were followed by large numbers of migrant compatriots, mostly merchants and traders who came to settle in Natal. A devoutly religious people, they brought their faith with them and built places of worship when they arrived.

For the most part, at first these were generally very simple and modest little shrines to serve the needs of single families — fashioned from whatever natural materials were available on the spot. But as the numbers of Hindu settlers grew and communities developed, their sacred buildings became larger, communal and more elaborate. The shrines were no longer makeshift buildings and grew more colourful and ornate, many on the lines of the Dravidian temple, the established traditional form in the south of India whence these workers had come to Natal.

Today the Indians are an established component of South Africa's population. There are now about 800 000 living in this country, mostly Hindu, but with about 20 per cent being Moslem.

Also from Asia have come numbers of Chinese. Just as Indians had been brought to work in the sugar industry in Natal, so were Chinese brought to South Africa early in the twentieth century as labour for the gold mines. As local black labour developed skills, however, most of the Chinese were repatriated. But, in the same way as Indian merchants had followed the early waves of workers to the sugar industry in Natal, so too the recruitment of these mine labourers brought Chinese merchants in its wake, adding yet further to the mosaic of nationalities and cultures in the developing country. Today about 11 000 people of Chinese descent are residents of South Africa.

While those first two-and-a-half centuries since Van Riebeeck's arrival in South Africa had seen the coming of various sects and religions from abroad, increasing numbers of the country's indigenous peoples, encouraged by Christian missionaries, were accepting the tenets and teachings of the imported religions.

The first organised missionary work among the black peoples began some 70 years after the arrival of the first ordained minister, though some bonded workers in individual households of the early Company officials and Dutch burghers were converted to the Christian faith. Since Christianity was a prerequisite for release from slave contract, it remains questionable whether Christianity or personal liberty was the real motive for acceptance of the faith.

History regards the Moravian, Georg Schmidt, as South Africa's first missionary. He came to the Cape in 1737 and worked among the Hottentots for seven years. It was not until almost 50 years later that three other Moravian missionaries, with the permission of the Dutch East India Company, arrived at the Cape and in 1792 re-established the mission station which a frustrated and disappointed Schmidt had abandoned. They named the place Genadendal — "Vale of Grace".

While of course not a church missionary in the accepted sense, Van Riebeeck might seem to have been the first European at the Cape to have been responsible for converting a locally born African from heathenism. His diary tells of the gradual acceptance of Christianity by Eva, a Hottentot teenager who served as his wife's maid and who, though not formally baptised, later herself went forth to spread Christianity among her people.

Having "learnt our language and partly our religion", Van Riebeeck's diary records on 29 October 1658, Eva decided not to return to her people "but to stay here for some while to learn more of our religion . . . "

The Moravians who resuscitated the activities at Genadendal towards the end of the eighteenth century were only some of many missionaries who, around the turn of that century, flocked to South Africa from countries of Europe to minister, first, to the Hottentots at the Cape and then, spreading out, to work among the Griquas and other peoples further north. Prominent among those organisations were the London Missionary Society and, in the Eastern Cape, the Wesleyans.

At the same time, in those early years of the nineteenth century, the Dutch Trekkers were establishing their churches wherever they settled across the Orange and, later, over the Vaal River. Their wish to be politically independent of the British-controlled Cape was echoed in their desire to be independent also of the mother church they had left behind. In practical terms the politics of continuing unity were aggravated by problems of contact and communication over the long distances and by the inability of the Cape Synod, itself short of ministers, to service the newly established Trekker congregations to the north.

Among the Trekkers themselves the secessionist issue generated considerable heat. Congregations in the Transvaal broke away from the Cape to form their own independent church administration, the Nederduitsch Hervormde Kerk, a move which was not unanimously accepted, however, and the congregation at Lydenburg remained linked with the church at the Cape.

Disruption did not end there, however, and within the Dutch church further splintering ensued. In 1859 at a meeting in Rustenburg, a group of Hervormde members broke away from the Transvaal group to establish the Gereformeerde Kerk (Reformed Church). Their members, which included Paul Kruger — later to become State President of the Transvaal Republic — objected to the singing of evangelical hymns in church on the grounds that hymns did not emanate from the Bible. They became known as "Doppers". The splintering did not end there, however. In 1866 a group formed itself into the Nederduitsch Gereformeerde Kerk in de Zuid-Afrikaansche Republiek.

Attempts over a number of years to re-unite the various segments of the Afrikaans Church have not proved successful, however, though some reconstruction of its ecclesiastical edifice has led to co-operation in various matters of common policy and concern.

In its earlier days in South Africa the so-called Anglican church was also not without certain divisive problems centring around the matter of administrative independence. Those came to a head when in 1876, after much wrangling and a decision by the Privy Council of Britain, the Church of the Province of Southern Africa was established as an autonomous body, independent of control by the Church of England in Britain. A branch of the Church of England continues to function separately in South Africa, however, with a current membership of about 100 000.

Official statistics indicate that more than 78 per cent of South Africa's population are Christians and that more than 20 per cent embrace indigenous African religions. Of the older Christian religions, the Dutch Reformed churches form the largest component, substantially larger than any others.

Of the traditionally established churches in South Africa, the Roman Catholic Church today has the next largest number of adherents, 80 per cent of whom are black. The early history of the Catholic church in South Africa was a somewhat chequered one. The practice of its faith was forbidden during the early years of the Dutch East India Company's rule at the Cape by an edict that only Protestants might live there, though services were clandestinely held in those years. But, notwithstanding the rescinding of the edict in 1804, Catholic priests who came to the Cape were ordered out of the country when the British took possession of the Cape in 1806. A Bishop appointed in 1818 by the Vatican to a large and scattered diocese which included the Cape was forced to live in Mauritius, though a priest was allowed to reside at the Cape. It was not until 1838 that a Catholic Bishop took up residence in the Cape Colony.

Despite those early difficulties, now long past, however, the Roman Catholic Church has made considerable headway in South Africa. Its contribution to the country's development has been especially significant in the field of education.

The Methodist Church has also built up a long and proud record of education in South Africa, not least in its contribution to the Xhosa language — including a translation of the Bible into Xhosa in 1859 — and in the training of black ministers in South Africa.

Many faiths, Christian and others — some large, some small — now have established places of worship in South Africa, benefiting the people of this country, both white and black, and winning souls for the traditional faiths of Europe and the East as well as the various new religions of the modern world. The pages of this book cannot hope to deal with more than a few of them by looking at some of the places of worship where those faiths are practised.

Africa, without established churches of its own, has long provided a fruitful field for missionary work and throughout the continent the results of the contacts between the indigenous people and the immigrants are becoming more and more manifest in the spread of the Moslem faith in the northern sectors of the continent, for example, and the rapid growth of Christianity in the south.

Nowhere in Africa in the twentieth century has this growth of religion among the indigenous people been more dramatic than in South Africa. This would seem perhaps to be a part of a broader — and universal — resurgence of religious faith.

In April 1989 *Time* magazine, writing about the vigorous growth of African art, said that though "Africa is a continent crucified by famine and war, pestilence and poverty, " it is, for Christianity, "a continent of resurrection." The report went on to point out that "even as older Christian churches in Europe and the U.S. are emptying, faith is thriving in the sprawling lands south of the Sahara." It has been estimated that each year recently some 600 000 people in Africa have turned to and accepted the Christian faith. That means more than one new Christian in Africa each minute!

This burgeoning of Christianity in Africa is generating a rich flowering of indigenous religious art, arguably unmatched in extent since the Renaissance in Europe. In this, South Africa is no exception. Examples proliferate, though the charm of its primitive, indigenous nature is fast tending to be diluted by close association with alien styles and popular modern influences.

The main thrust of this movement in South Africa is to be seen also in the establishment and development of separate independent black churches, of which there are now several thousand, all wholly independent of the traditional churches from which many of them have seceded but whose procedures and faiths, routines and customs they still follow and practise, albeit, often, in diluted and modified forms.

The sudden increase in the numbers of these churches and sects in South Africa in recent years must be seen as an acceleration of a movement from heathenism towards Christianity which began a long while ago — indeed, it might be said, with the conversion of a servant in the household of Van Riebeeck himself. For a long while, however, religious teaching remained in the hands of whites, and three centuries were to pass before Africans themselves began to take on the role of religious teaching and administration. A school inaugurated in 1853 by the Wesleyans at Healdtown in the eastern Cape for Africans and given a grant of 3 000 pounds by the British Government began the training of African teachers and ministers. In 1880 the theological training was moved to Lesseyton. It was the first institution in the country especially for the religious training of Africans and may thus be said to be the fountainhead of black Christian religion in South Africa.

The next step in the growth of independent black churches in South Africa came not much later. About 1886 a small self-governing church was formed in Tembuland, its adherents becoming Baptists. A similar separatist church, following Wesleyan lines, set itself up in Johannesburg soon afterwards and became known as "the Ethiopian Church", not on account of any links or affiliations with Ethiopia, but rather because Ethiopia was then the only black, free and independent country in an otherwise colonial-controlled continent. The separatist church movement in South Africa took on the appellation of "Ethiopian".

Without doubt the largest and strongest independent religious movement in South Africa today is that of the Zionists — whose designation comes not from any links with Jewish Zionism, but derives rather from the movement of that name established by the Reverend John Alexander Dowie of Zion City, Illinois, in the United States soon after the turn of this century. In South Africa Zionism had its beginnings at Wakkerstroom (q.v.) in about 1900.

Several thousand of the proliferating independent modern charismatic African churches throughout the country today incorporate the word "Zion" in their names in one form or another.

In general, while expressive of African claims, these churches tend to follow the liturgy of the white churches and use similar forms of service, free, however, of much of the dogma entrenched in tradition. Considerably influenced by twentieth century Pentecostal religious developments in the United States, the beliefs of many of these Christian sects embrace healing by faith and baptism by immersion.

Among those many African Zionist movements the largest and most prominent is that of the Zionist Christian Church, now split into two organisations — both large — which have their headquarters side by side at Moria (q.v.) near Pietersburg in the northern Transvaal.

In the growth and development of South Africa the diverse and multiracial nature of its peoples has led — inevitably — to numbers of problems through the years. But the very diversity of the population holds promise of a rich cultural future in the unified society which one day will emerge, tempered perhaps in the fires of political conflict along the way.

This broad promise — this hope — becomes especially manifest in the field of religion in South Africa. There is a ready acceptance by communities of the religions and religious rights of other groups and, whatever religious wars and conflicts may disturb the peace and social tranquillity in other parts of the world and whatever political feuds may erupt into flame in South Africa, religious communities, in which differences of creed, race and colour no longer exist, live peacefully side by side throughout the land.

34 The Groote Kerk
Cape Town

37 The Cathedral Church of
St George the Martyr
Cape Town

40 The Gardens Synagogues
Cape Town

43 Nederduitse Gereformeerde Kerk
Graaff-Reinet

46 The Roman Catholic Mission
Pella

49 The Moffat Mission
Kuruman

52 The Methodist Commemoration Church
Grahamstown

55 The Cathedral of Christ the King
Queenstown

57 The Cathedral of St Michael
and St George
Grahamstown

60 The Holy Trinity Church
Belvidere

63 The Sheikh Yusuf Kramat
Faure

66 The Synagogue
Kimberley

69 The Moravian Mission
Mamre

72 Mission Church of the Holy Cross
Mackay's Nek

75 Nederduitse Gereformeerde Kerk
Cradock

79 The Yellowwood Church of St Andrew
Redbourne

81 The Rhenish Church
Stellenbosch

84 St Patrick on the Hill
Hogsback

86 The Myrtle Rigg Church
Bonnievale

88 St Luke's: A Private Chapel
Onrus

(Facing page)

*Rose window in the south transept
of the Cathedral of St George the Martyr,
Cape Town; created by Francis Spear*

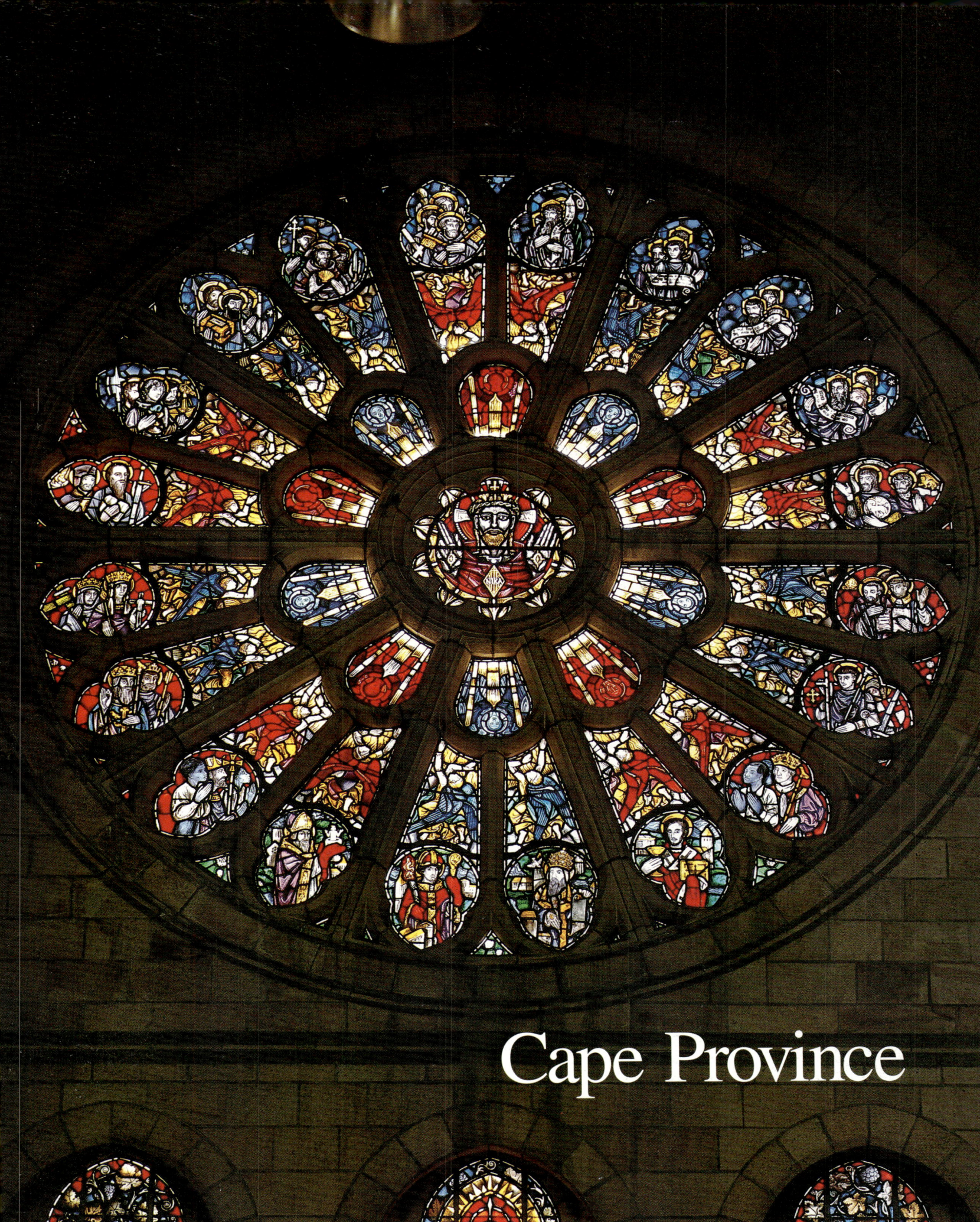
Cape Province

The Groote Kerk
Cape Town

(Left)
Memorial stone set into the wall of the Groote Kerk, Cape Town

The first church service held at the Cape took place, not ashore, but on one of the ships of Van Riebeeck's small fleet eight days after his arrival in Table Bay. On that occasion "... after Sunday service," his Journal reports, "we went with all the boats to the Salt River to fish..." From the records the first Sunday service ashore would seem to have been held a fortnight later when — there being no resident ordained minister — the "Sick-comforter" offered prayers and read a sermon.

The first full-scale church service at the Cape took place, however, about five weeks after the arrival of those first Company officials when a minister from a passing ship happened to be available and on "a beautiful day with a N.W. breeze," as Van Riebeeck's Journal records, "... in the still uncovered part of the house inside the square of the unfinished fort, everybody standing, the Reverend Backerius... held the first sermon, and the Lord's Supper was celebrated..."

For some while after that, in those early years of European settlement, the Company held church services, first, in a hall in the Fort and, later, in a converted shed in the Castle which had been made available. Then in 1675 a small church was built within the precincts of the Castle and used for the following 20 years until the minister pleaded for a new church. Nothing had come of a planned place of worship for which the foundations had already been laid. Later, in 1700, however, those were dug up and work began in earnest on the building of a church outside the Castle's walls on ground which

(Below)
The Church Square entrance to the Groote Kerk

(Below)
The old tower, built in 1701.
The clock was originally installed in 1771

for some years had served as a graveyard. Provision was made for prominent persons to be interred inside the new church.

It was opened in January 1704, a fine steepled building with an ornate pulpit. The need for increased seating to accommodate the growing congregation led to several alterations and extensions in the following 130 years. At that stage, the old structure being no longer safe, it was demolished to make way for a new building into which the original (1703) baroque tower of the old place of worship was incorporated. A four-faced chiming clock was installed in the tower in 1771.

Several gravestones of nine governors and several well-known personages who had been buried in the former cemetery were inlaid in the

(Below)
Lithograph of the Groote Kerk,
produced by J.H. Poorteman, circa 1835

floor of the church and others were set in the north wall where their inscriptions may still be read.

That building — which still serves the community — was inaugurated in January 1841. It remains South Africa's senior church and one continuing the fine traditions it inherited, its congregation sharing in the history that covers the whole period of European settlement in the country.

In the flourishing centre of one of the country's capital cities, it is now dwarfed by buildings which have grown up around it so that its venerable beauty cannot be fully appreciated. Some years ago the Council of the Groote Kerk wisely erected a building on the northern side, not least to protect the old church and the historic tower.

The plainness of its spacious interior is relieved by the beauty of the ornamental rosettes on its vaulted ceiling and by the grandeur of the large baroque pulpit carved by the German, Anton Anreith, from a single block of wood and installed in 1779. With a base of intricately carved lions and with a fine canopy, its size emphasises its magnificence and makes it the dominant feature of the church.

The seniority and its location in one of South Africa's capital cities has led to the Groote Kerk's being used for a number of State occasions.

(Above)
Stucco ornamentation on the domed ceiling

(Left)
Pulpit carved by Anton Anreith and Jan Jacob and inaugurated in 1789

The Cathedral of St George the Martyr
Cape Town

It is only to be expected that, as the Dutch settled at the Cape more than a century and a half before any other nation made its mark there, the first alien places of worship in that region would be theirs. Though Jan van Riebeeck built the first — inside the Fort — soon after his arrival, the oldest church still in existence at the Cape is the well-known Groote Kerk (q.v.) at the top of Adderley Street. It was opened 52 years after Van Riebeeck's arrival and 100 years before the British took over the administration of the Cape. But even before then, English people were living there, though without a church of their own.

That was not to say, however, that the initial lack of a church deprived the growing English community at the Cape of the opportunity of collective worship. For many years a felicitous arrangement with the Dutch Church authorities enabled the English to worship in the Groote Kerk.

Today, within a few hundred metres of the Groote Kerk, at the entrance to the Gardens, stands the Anglican Cathedral of St George the Martyr, the site for which was consecrated in October 1827, two decades after the institution of British administration. The first service in its precincts was held in 1834, and, with the arrival of Robert Gray, the first Bishop of Cape Town, in 1848 the church became a cathedral.

St George's was not the first English-speaking place of worship at the Cape, however. It was preceded by St Andrew's Presbyterian Church, which was dedicated in May 1829.

Gray is said to have been happy neither with the modest size of the building nor with its design, which was modelled on the church of St Pancras in London. His belief that Cape Town deserved a finer cathedral was shared by many and more than two decades later his successor was of much the same

(Above)
The Cross, near the west entrance, is from the old St George's Cathedral

(Left)
The Cathedral, seen from Wale Street, circa 1900

A:M D:G
THIS STONE WAS LAID BY
H.R.H GEORGE DUKE
OF CORNWALL AND YORK
22ND AUGUST A.D. 1901

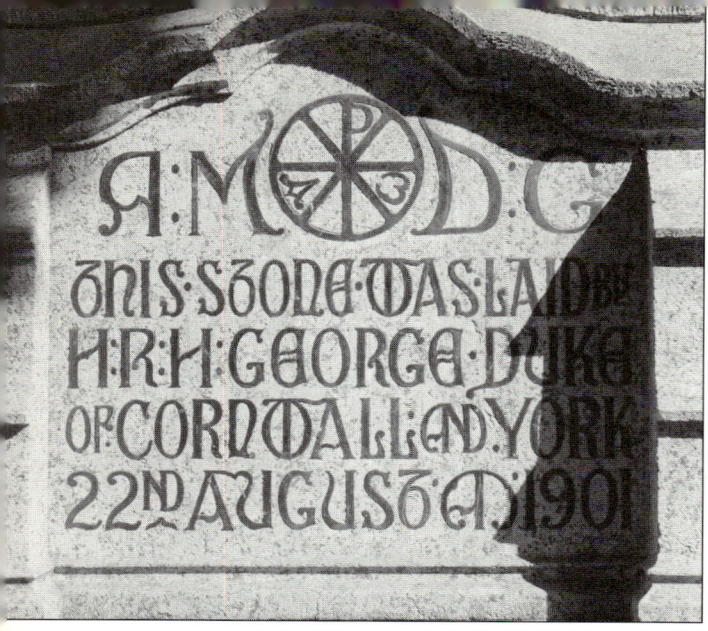

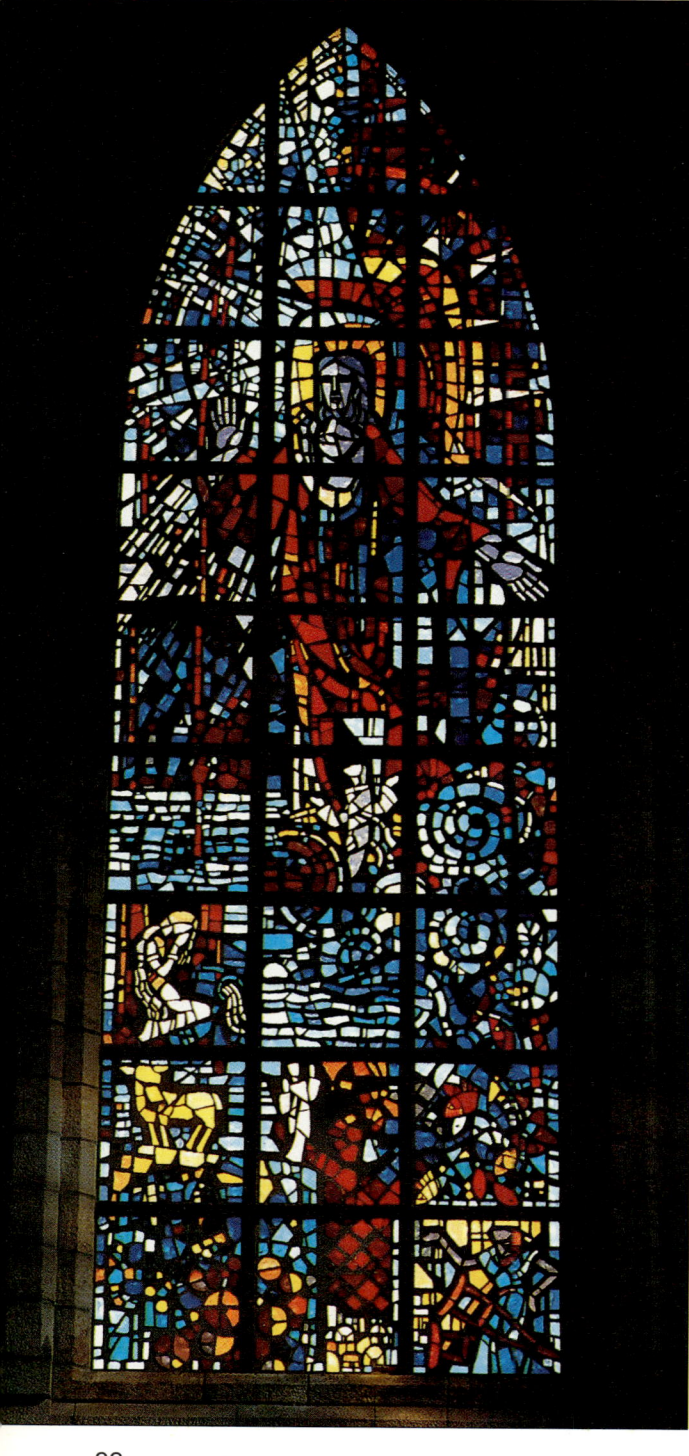

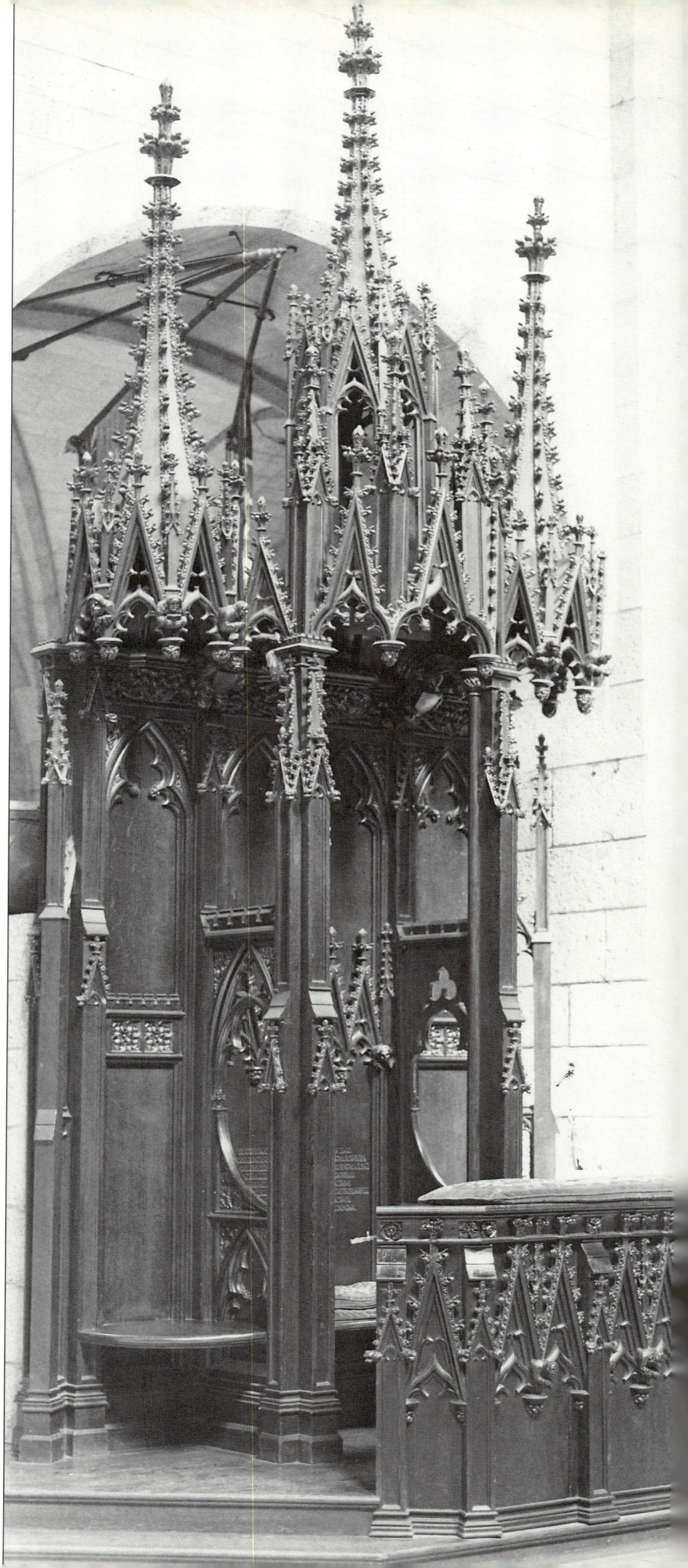

(Far left above)
The foundation stone of the present cathedral, laid in August 1901 by the Duke of Cornwall and York, later to become King George V

(Far left below)
Stained-glass window of the Ascension, created by Mayer of Munich: one of a set of eight made in 1886 for the old cathedral. It is a memorial to Bishop Robert Gray

(Centre)
The Archbishop's Throne, made from the choir screen of Westminster Abbey

(Left)
The rood above the sanctuary

opinion. Schemes for a new cathedral were proposed but made no headway, until, towards the end of the century, plans for a new building were drawn by Herbert Baker and the foundation stone was laid in 1901. After delays caused by the South African war, work commenced on the construction of a new cathedral — one in more imposing Gothic style.

Progress was slow and there were many interruptions, so that it was only in 1936, after alterations and additions, that Herbert Baker's grand design began to be seen.

Today, almost 160 years after the site was consecrated, the Cathedral Church of St George the Martyr is still not complete. Plans await funds to implement them. In the intervening years several bishops have come and gone. The Church of England in this country, now independent of Canterbury, has become the Church of the Province of South Africa. A bishop's diocese has been elevated to an archbishopric and the Cathedral in Cape Town is its seat.

The building is a fine one and doubtless, in its continuing march to completion, further additions will add to its grandeur, much of it now unfortunately concealed, however, by interfering commercial buildings which tend to complicate a view of the Cathedral as a whole. A pity! But the splendour of the interior remains unaffected. Its soaring roof, the moving beauty of the many fine stained-glass windows and the glory of the gilded rood high above the Sanctuary — these are among the visible treasures which make the historic Cathedral of St George memorable.

The Gardens Synagogues
Cape Town

(Right)
The Great Synagogue, set among the oak trees of Cape Town's historic Gardens

(Far right above)
The new synagogue, adjacent to the old place of worship which is now the Jewish Museum

(Far right below)
The east façade of the synagogue

While the tall twin towers of Cape Town's Great Synagogue stand silhouetted against the rocky majesty of Table Mountain, peering quietly over the trees in the city's historic Gardens, the older place of Jewish worship, close at its side, stands hidden from passers-by, concealed by those same oaks in the parkland that was first set aside in 1652 for growing vegetables to keep ships' crews healthy on the long voyages between Holland and the East.

Though non-Protestants were prohibited from living at the Cape for the first 150 years of European settlement, it is reasonably certain that the population in those early years did include a small — unknown — number of Jews who, for obvious reasons, concealed their religious affiliations. But it was not until almost four decades after the lifting of the Protestants-only ban that the Jews made any move towards organising a body of their own, when in 1841 they founded the Society of the Jewish Community of Cape Town.

Initially their religious services were held in Jewish homes, but in 1849 premises were bought and altered for use as a synagogue. Later that year the arrival from England of the first Rabbi, the Reverend Isaac Pulver, formally set the seal on the existence of a Jewish community and congregation in Cape Town.

From the outset these premises were not intended to be anything but temporary and it was clear that the building would be replaced sooner or later by some more permanent and appropriate place of worship. The growth of the congregation crystallised this need and in 1861 it was decided to build a synagogue and, too, a house for the minister.

Almost precisely a year later, when funds had been raised and property purchased, the foundation stone was laid and a further year later, with great ceremony, the new synagogue was consecrated — and South Africa had its very first *Shul*.

A visitor to Cape Town in 1894 wrote: "... The Jewish Synagogue is picturesquely situated in the Avenue, and was opened in 1863. The cost was 2 400 pounds. The pastor lives in an adjoining house, the property of the community..."

That synagogue — no longer used as a place of worship — was built in neo-Egyptian style, with lotus-flower capitals to the columns. As an architectural style it enjoyed brief popularity in Europe at the time, but the vogue was short-lived and had a very limited following in South Africa.

With the considerable influx of Jews to the country in the latter decades of the last century, the synagogue soon became too small and after extensions had proved to be of short-lived usefulness, it was decided to build a new place of Jewish worship on the ground alongside the Old *Shul*.

Sir Walter Hely-Hutchinson, Governor of the Cape, laid the foundation stone in 1904 and in September of the following year the Great Synagogue was consecrated. It is a fine building of considerable dignity and impressive proportions — both inside and out — with decoration that relieves the plainness of the airy and spacious interior under a large stucco dome, yet is restrained enough to maintain the quiet, solemn dignity of this holy place.

Moderation in the ornamentation serves to emphasise the beauty of the mosaic work in the semi-circular apse where the Ark is housed and concentrates attention on the fine carving and the polished wood of the pulpit.

In 1946 the little synagogue, cheek by jowl with its younger relation, became the Jewish Museum, displaying treasures which record aspects of the history of the Hebrews, both in South Africa and elsewhere. Much of the Old *Shul* remains untouched, with the beauty of parts unimpaired by the change of status. Among the vestiges of its past are the magnificent stained-glass windows installed in 1884 in the apse, above the Ark, memorials to Sir Moses Montefiore who contributed so much to the Jewish community of the Cape.

*(Left)
Stained-glass windows,
a memorial to Sir Moses
Montefiore*

Nederduitse Gereformeerde Kerk
Graaff-Reinet

The impressive Dutch Reformed Church dominates this Karoo town from all angles

Few indeed would dispute that this magnificent Dutch Reformed Church in Graaff-Reinet is among the noblest and most splendid places of worship in South Africa. Set centrally in a town itself brimming with buildings of architectural beauty as well as great historical interest, the church — emblazoned with the symbol of the National Monuments Council — presides proudly over the Karoo town, quiet and confident in the self-knowledge of its own dignity and splendour. Its lofty tower and tapering spire gaze across the far widths of the hills, mountains and the plains of the surrounding landscape.

By South African standards it is a venerable and historic building, now more than a hundred years old. The present building is the fourth to have served the local Dutch Reformed congregation and the third to have occupied this central site in the town. The cornerstone was laid in April 1886, almost a century after the establishment of the original congregation and the building of its first little church.

That stone was laid by the widow of the great Dr Andrew Murray, a Scots minister who answered a call from the Dutch church in the Cape Colony and who came to Graaff-Reinet in 1822 to be minister there until his death in 1866. One of his sons, the Reverend Charles Murray, was appointed in his place.

It was during Charles Murray's tenure of office that the size of the congregation was found to have outgrown the capacity of the existing building so that a bigger church became necessary. By 1885 sufficient money had been raised for the purpose and, after the demolition of the *"klein kerkie"*, construction of a new — and larger — church

(Left)
The early morning light strikes Spandau Kop above Graaff-Reinet

(Right)
This Bible, printed in 1741, forms part of the church's fine collection of historic treasures

began. To distinguish it from its predecessor, the new church became known as *"die Grootkerk"*.

The stone for its construction was quarried on Neser's farm, close to Graaff-Reinet. It was cut and prepared by the owner who donated the dressed stone to the building fund, the cash amount of R25 000 of which was augmented by many such contributions in kind. The money, it turned out, was insufficient to meet the final building costs of R36 000, however.

Bisset, a Cape Town architect, was appointed to design the church and the firm of Grant and Downie was appointed to build it.

It was consecrated in September 1887.

The completed church is arguably the finest example of Victorian Gothic architecture in South Africa, with its lines and features, its pointed Gothic arches and windows splendidly delineated and emphasised in stonework of a lighter, contrasting colour. The building is capped at its southern end by a tall tapering white steeple that beckons across the town beneath and far across the surrounding countryside.

The stonework around some of the windows is embellished by the addition of interesting small carved heads, male and female, both crowned, the significance of which remains the secret of the designer.

The interior is spacious and airy; the absence of ornamentation emphasising the simplicity of its internal form. The gallery at the rear, with its large and ornate organ, installed in 1894, spreads across the width of the nave. The angled ceiling of wood is supported by rounded beams of kiaat. The plain white walls and the clear undecorated windows enhance the quality of the light within the building, magnifying the sense of spaciousness. Galleries in the transepts on either side of the magnificently carved pulpit augment the seating capacity.

Tucked away among the gables, cleverly concealed from casual view, is a chimney — unusual in a church building. Indeed, this church in Graaff-Reinet is said to be the only Dutch Reformed Church in South Africa to have a fireplace in its committee room! It has never been used, however.

Among the treasured possessions accumulated by the congregation in the two centuries of its existence are several historic old Bibles and a unique collection of valuable church silver, much of it made by early silversmiths at the Cape.

The Roman Catholic Mission
Pella

*(Left)
A glimpse of the barren, rocky and desolate environment surrounding Pella*

In Hebrew the word *Pella* means "miracle" and while the name of the mission station in northern Namaqualand does not derive directly from that — and nor is the mission there Jewish — many would aver that the continuing existence of a settlement in an environment so inhospitable to man might itself be seen as something of a miracle. For more than a century and a half the mission has endured not only droughts and a cruel climate, but has also lived through several wars which have brushed past it.

Created in travail, Pella is a remarkable place with a significant history and a record of proud achievement.

The Roman Catholic Mission, with its fine cathedral, lies beside a straggling village in a dusty bowl amid grim, dark rocky mountains which tower above it. These mountains were described by Thompson, the English explorer who visited the area in 1824, as "rising in frowning grandeur, almost perpendicular" to the height of about 2 000 feet above the "desolate station" which, when he reached there, he found abandoned on account of the prevailing drought.

These mountains, with their rocky canyons and deep ravines, separate the settlement from the Orange River, a few kilometres to the north, which here now forms a segment of the boundary between South Africa and Namibia.

In 1806 the London Missionary Society set up a station, its first across the Orange River, at Warmbad, a little more than 70 kilometres northwest of Pella in what is now Namibia. In 1811, a tribal feud between the Hottentots at the mission and the local chief, Jager Afrikaner, led to the ransacking of the station. Its inhabitants fled across the Orange River and came to rest at Cammas Fonteyn where, under Christian Albrecht, they established a new mission station, giving it the name Pella after the town in ancient Palestine to which persecuted Christians had fled in 70 AD when Jerusalem was destroyed by the Romans under Titus.

Daunted by the harassment of the Bushmen, who murdered several of the newcomers, and by the ravages of the heat and drought which seasonally destroyed all grazing, these Christians were soon compelled to abandon the station, which was then closed down by the London Missionary Society. The Rhenish Mission took possession of the place but after a while, in 1869, they too abandoned it. Five years later the Roman Catholics took over the place and, their occupancy formally recognised in 1881, they have been there ever since.

The first priests there, Father Gaudeul and Brother George, were soon replaced by four French priests of the Order of St Francis de Sales. Unaccustomed to a lonely desert environment, two soon returned to France, while another left not long afterwards. This left the young Father Simon to carry on alone — until replacements arrived: two priests and three nuns. One of the nuns became a victim of sunstroke and went back to Europe.

Helped by an encyclopaedia of arts and crafts, the priests — with no experience of building — set to to build houses and schools and, later, a cathedral.

Under the direction of Father Simon, work on the cathedral began in 1886. First, 1 260 wagonloads of earth were brought to level the site. Then more than 400 wagonloads of stone were used in laying the foundations and 200 000 bricks were made beside the Orange River and carted to the

site at a rate of 500 bricks a day. Three hundred sacks of lime were dug to supply plaster. It was a monumental task.

While Brother Wolf and his workers chopped wood for the beams — on an island more than 80 kilometres away in the Orange River — they were frequently attacked by baboons.

For years the work went on. Progress was slow and not without setbacks. In 1888 some 30 000 bricks were lost when, in the hot, drought-stricken area, the Orange River flooded after heavy rains in the Transvaal, far upstream.

But eventually the task was completed and the cathedral proclaimed the splendour of the achievement. In August 1895, after several months of delay caused by drought, the cathedral was consecrated before a huge crowd who had come from far and wide and who were treated — most for the first time in their lives — to a display of home-made fireworks whose eccentric performances added unplanned excitement to the occasion.

The cathedral is an impressive building, elegantly proportioned, in what might be described as French colonial style: inside, stout white-painted stone columns separate the central nave from the aisles; transepts — with small chapels — give the building its cruciform shape. An ornate altar graces a colourful apse.

Outside, the plainness of the walls of the long rectangular building is relieved by buttresses, while over the porch at the main entrance there is a tall clock-tower and spire. From an alcove in the tower a painted statue of Christ looks out across the dusty acres of the churchyard.

In the north chapel are buried the fathers of this cathedral. Among them are Bishop Simon and Father Wolf, whose hands and minds fashioned this sanctuary. They lie at rest in the place they created for the God and the people they served.

The cathedral and surrounding school buildings are set among palm trees whose green fronds not only give shade, but also relieve the drab khaki of the arid landscape. The fruit of these palms is popular and sales country-wide bring revenue to the mission. The origins of this minor industry are not without interest.

In the campaign against German South West Africa during the First World War, a detachment of South African troops camped at Pella *en route* to the German territory. Dates formed a part of their rations, and from the discarded seeds trees grew — the beginning of an industry which has since been developed by the acquisition of cultivars from the United States.

Here, in this quiet valley protected by the awesome, bare rocky mountains which form an impressive backdrop to the settlement, the life of this Christian mission flows quietly on, contented in its solitude. Here each hour is a gentle sample of eternity: each passing day merely the quiet tick of some infinite time-piece.

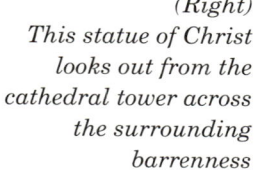

*(Right)
This statue of Christ looks out from the cathedral tower across the surrounding barrenness*

The Moffat Mission
Kuruman

(Below)
Geese enjoy Moffat's furrow which brings water to the mission from Kuruman's "Eye"

The "Eye" at Kuruman, a perennial spring in a rocky outcrop, produces between 18- and 20-million litres of cool fresh water daily in an otherwise arid region, and is remarkably little affected by the long dry spells which frequently beset that area of the north-eastern Cape. It is the source of a river which the Bushmen, the first settlers there, named "Kuruan", from which the town derives its name.

The reliability and abundance of the water supply made the place ideal for settlement and in 1801 Jan Kok and William Edwards of the London Missionary Society decided to establish a mission station there among the Batlhaping tribe who controlled that area. Their efforts proved abortive, however. Kok was murdered not long after their arrival and Edwards, disheartened and discouraged, went back to Cape Town.

Further attempts by the Society to work with the Batlhaping proved similarly unsuccessful and it was not until Robert Moffat took control in 1821 that the mission station gave any impression of being there to stay, an impression which was strengthened when Moffat, pointing out to Chief Mothibi the possibility of irrigating the river valley, persuaded him of the advantages which would accrue.

It was not until 1824, however, that the missionaries were able to begin working on the scheme at a point some 4 kilometres from the Eye on land granted by the tribal Chief and where the mission was set up anew. It is where the church stands today.

Near the Eye Moffat and his compatriot, Hamilton, built a dam, labouring on the project themselves. From there they dug a furrow, 2 metres wide, which they lined with clay to lead the water 4 kilometres to the area selected for cultivation. The results of the work — which took almost two years — are to be seen today, as is Moffat's house, the oldest building north of the Orange River. A school was also built and opened.

But while the construction of the mission station progressed, achievement in the religious field was discouragingly absent. Christian instruction brought no converts, and, even more distressing, prevailing attitudes among the Africans provided little hope for such success; until, suddenly, in July 1829 the curtain of indifference was rent and the first six Batswana offered themselves for baptism.

Three of the converts soon made manifest their new Christian spirit by volunteering to build a school at the mission — and to pay for it themselves.

Encouraged by such developments, Moffat and his fellow missionaries began building a church. They lined up its front with the frontage of Moffat's

(Left)
The mission church built by Robert Moffat

(Below left)
The stump of the almond tree under which David Livingstone proposed to Mary Moffat

(Far right)
Sunshine and shadows play on the doorway of Moffat's church

(Right)
Bronze plaque of Robert Moffat at the mission

(Below)
An old hour-glass stands on the altar table to time the preacher's sermon

homestead, close to the furrow, to mark the edge of the road which would — they anticipated — one day be the main highway from Cape Town to the interior of Africa.

The building was — and is — a large one, its size a mark of faith. Moffat designed it to seat 800 people at a time when he had only nine converts! Moffat described it as a simple structure "without steeple or gallery", and it remains thus today. Building took many years. The thick stone walls stood roofless for seven years before timber sufficiently large and stout was located for the making of the necessary beams. Hugh Millen, a Scots stonemason, died while scouring the countryside for timber. The wood, brought by ox-wagon from 350 kilometres away, came from Marico in the Transvaal.

The church remains as Moffat wished it to be: plain and simple. There is no ceiling to the high thatched roof and the exposed supporting beams give character to the interior. The earthen floor is smeared with dung, while near the stone font and pulpit platform the floor is paved with slate. The

wooden windows, white-painted, have small panes, plain and without decoration, admitting gentle light without upsetting the cool of the airy interior.

Beside the lectern is a wrought-iron candle-holder to which is chained an old-fashioned hourglass, to time the preacher's sermon.

This historic building, a National Monument, now serves as the central church of the United Congregational Church in the region.

Together with a number of other buildings, it stands among leafy trees, indigenous syringas and exotic oaks, with Mary Moffat's garden green beside the furrow of fast-flowing water from the Eye. Here stands the old and wizened stump of the almond tree under which David Livingstone proposed to Mary, daughter of Robert and Mary Moffat.

Close by, beneath a gnarled oak, rests the old ox-wagon used by the early missionaries in their trips to outlying tribal villages.

Under Robert Moffat, the mission at Kuruman became the most famous in all Africa. It was important not only for its religious achievements — and eventually those were many — but also as an early outpost of European civilisation and culture in southern Africa, becoming a base from which these cultural values flowed into the central regions of the continent. It was from here, too, that David Livingstone and other explorers set out on their journeys deeper into Africa.

Because it was the water from the Eye which led to the establishment of this famous mission station, that source of the Kuruman River is often described as the fountain of Christianity in Africa.

The Methodist Commemoration Church
Grahamstown

A look at Grahamstown today makes it difficult to believe that it was once the second largest town in southern Africa.

It developed from a military cantonment to a small settlement that grew in size suddenly with the arrival of the 1820 settlers, brought from England to strengthen the eastern Cape defences against the Xhosas. But, although in size today overtaken by several major ports and towns, Grahamstown retains its old charm, untainted by the rush and bustle of bigger cities.

Something — at least — of that charm must be attributed to its many handsome Victorian buildings, while much of the quiet, unhurried atmosphere stems from the presence of a large university and several major schools and colleges. In relation to its size, an unusually large number of churches there have earned Grahamstown the sobriquet of "the city of saints".

One of these many places of worship is the beautiful red-sandstone Methodist church, widely referred to as the "Commem" Church from the fact that it was built to commemorate the blessings conferred by God on the first generation of those hardy British 1820 settlers.

Gothic in style, the Commemoration Church stands in the centre of Grahamstown at the lower end of the Church Square that is dominated by the tall Anglican Cathedral (q.v) higher up and by the sturdy tower of the town hall close by.

While a place of worship must essentially always be a part of the community it serves, at the same time (many would argue) its sanctity and chastity demand a certain respectful physical isolation from other man-made elements around it. Commem's main doorway is directly on the street itself and the church appears cramped by intruding buildings.

Windows facing the square are Gothic, tall and narrow, with moulded pointed arches. The façade is ornamented by stepped buttresses topped by decorated pinnacles.

The foundation stone was laid in April 1845 — the "Silver Jubilee" of the arrival of those British settlers — and the first service in the church was held in November five years later. It was designed to accommodate 1 200 worshippers, that number embracing the entire population of Grahamstown at the time.

"Commem" was not the first Methodist place of worship to be built in Grahamstown, however. The first chapel, dedicated in November 1822 — soon after the arrival of the settlers — was used also by other denominations for a number of years. Despite being enlarged twice, that first church soon proved too small and another was built in 1832 — the inadequacy of which, in turn, led to the building of the Commemoration Church.

Its interior is rectangular. Box pews face the altar-table, behind which is the organ — said to be one of the finest in the country. Beneath the stepped, plaster ceiling a gallery runs along three sides, supported by slender metal pillars.

The backs and seats of the pews in the gallery are incised with a confusion of names of generations of schoolboys. Clearly it was fashionable to engrave one's name there and the carvings — most with more panache than art and skill — are not seen as desecration but rather have become accepted as a feature of the church!

There are nobler epitaphs, however, certainly more decorously presented. Many tablets of distinction and beauty in both brass and marble grace the walls of the historic church, paying tribute to the founders of this place of worship and to the labours of those who developed the city of Grahamstown.

But the most beautiful of the attractions of the Commem church are undoubtedly its many magnificent stained-glass windows, best known of which is the "Settlers' Window" in the north-west corner, depicting the arrival of the first settlers.

The inscription beneath, taken from the Gospel of St Luke 10:3 — "Behold, I send you forth in the midst of wolves" — is an apt reminder of the political situation of the area prevailing in 1820 when the settlers came to the eastern Cape and, by their presence, created a bulwark against the marauding Xhosas.

This Methodist "Commem" Church is much beloved: a proud monument to the courage and fortitude, the travail and endeavours of those early settlers.

(Far left) The front of the "Commem" church on the High Street

(Left) The "Settlers' Window" in the Methodist Commemoration Church

*(Right)
Mosaic of Christ the King, created by Sister Pientia Selhorst, situated behind the altar. The mosaic panel measures 6,20 by 3,41 metres*

The Cathedral of Christ the King
Queenstown

Two of several places of worship in Queenstown may be said to be especially significant for the magnificence of the art which decorates and beautifies their respective interiors. One is St Michael's Anglican Church; the other is the Roman Catholic Cathedral of Christ the King.

The town is fortunate indeed to possess treasures — spiritual as well as visual — of such rich worth.

These two places of worship differ in many respects. Architecturally each represents a different age. St Michael's — built in the nineteenth century — has its architectural roots in earlier tradition, built of stone and with stained-glass windows in classical style. By contrast the cathedral is modern, with gentle angularity in its design, and is clearly a product of the twentieth century.

But both are beautiful — with visual and spiritual beauty that also emphasises the splendour of the ornamentation within their walls.

The cathedral, consecrated in 1959, is an imposing building which, from a broad natural terrace above a trickling, winding river, overlooks much of the sprawling town and surrounding countryside.

Its external plainness and an absence of ornamentation on its concrete construction gives an impression of solidarity, of a firmness of resolve and a strength of purpose, all made benevolent, however, by the warmth generated by the sunny colouring of its walls.

A tall plain tower rises starkly above the entrance on the south side. On the façade above the entrance porch a large mosaic panel depicts the coat of arms of the Bishop who held office at the time of the cathedral's consecration.

Two bronze handles to the large main doors, also of bronze, are shaped as dragon's heads, artistically executed in the tradition of using representations of fiendish beasts on places of worship to keep evil spirits at bay.

The contemporary style is made further manifest within the building by the way in which the liturgical needs have been met, reflecting modern thinking in ecclesiastical architecture.

(Below)
The cathedral on the hill overlooking the stream and park

The interior is almost square, with the altar in the centre, not only closer to the congregation, but also positioned so that all worshippers may enjoy a greater sense of participation in proceedings. The altar itself has been created from local sandstone, its front decorated by a large plaque, in beaten silver, of a representation of the Lamb of God.

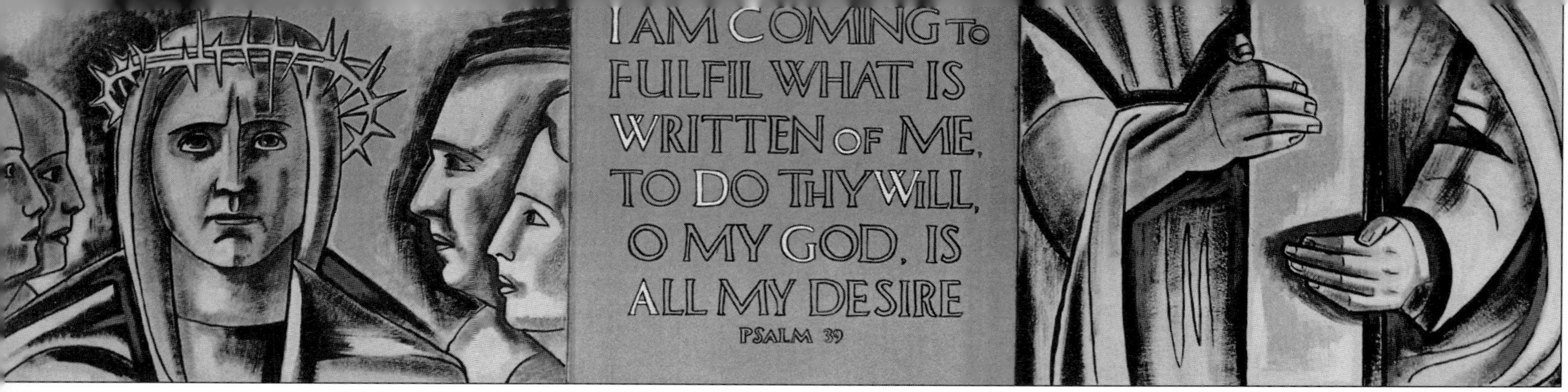

A gallery around three sides is supported by square pillars which reach to the domed ceiling, the main source of internal lighting. The other windows are small and elongated with stained glass comprising contemporary abstract designs by Sister Pientia Selhorst, a Dutch artist who took Holy Orders and whose work decorates a number of Roman Catholic places of worship in South Africa. The windows were made in Germany.

A magnificent large mosaic panel, almost 6 metres in height, dominates the interior and is flanked by two equally beautiful narrower mosaic panels of similar height.

The central panel depicts Christ the King, one hand raised in blessing, the other holding a lily. The panel to the right depicts Mary, her hands in prayer. The other panel shows John the Baptist, the precursor of Christ, which is felt to be appropriate in a land where missionary work is important.

These panels, too, are the work of Sister Pientia Selhorst, whose artistic skill and sensitivity also created the moving and unusual frieze of the Stations of the Cross which adorns the walls beneath the gallery. It is painted directly on the walls with an economy of line and a subtle use of colour that generate powerful emotions and a force which emphasises Christ's suffering on His way to the Cross.

The cathedral was designed by Ivan Barac, a local architect, whose plans won an open competition which attracted a considerable number of entries, several from overseas.

Not only functional in contemporary terms, this Cathedral of Christ the King, with its rich art, imbues worship with a deeper dimension.

(Above) Details of part of the frieze of the Stations of the Cross; designed and executed by Sister Pientia Selhorst

(Below) The Lamb of God; a plaque in beaten silver on the front of the altar

The Cathedral of St Michael and St George
Grahamstown

The martial background to the founding of Grahamstown is encapsulated in the name of the fine Anglican cathedral there, recalling its two warrior guardians — the sword-bearing St Michael, conqueror of Satan, and the soldier-lancer St George, Patron Saint of England, who slayed the evil dragon.

Nor does the military association end there.

The memorials and monuments which adorn the cathedral's interior themselves provide — in their way as much as any pages from a history book — an account of the origins and development of the town and record the roles of many of the men and women who helped found it.

On the right, just inside the main entrance under the soaring Gothic tower, is a marble memorial to the British soldier Colonel John Graham, "Commandant of Simons Town", whose military headquarters in operations on the Cape's eastern borders in 1814 became a town named after him.

The military influence of the passing years is to be seen also in the memorials to the fallen in various conflicts: in the Basuto War of 1880-81, for example, as well as in the Bechuanaland Campaign of 1897 — "Erected by the Comrades in the Bechuana Field Force", and to those who fell in action in "the disastrous war of 1846..." Another plaque honours those from Grahamstown who were members of South Africa's forces in the campaign in German East Africa in 1916-17: those who served in France in 1914-18 are elsewhere remembered too. Another memorial, carved in wood, recalls the war of 1939-45: "In honour of those men and women from this Parish who served in the World War and in memory of those who did not return. May they rest in peace."

But interest is not limited to historic military matters. The beauty of many fine stained-glass windows supplements the grandeur of the architecture.

St George's began as a parish church, its construction financed by the British government. Though building commenced in 1824, on the site of the old military parade ground, it was not until six years later that services were first held there. In 1834 the building served as a place of refuge for women and children during the Sixth Frontier War. It then consisted of one room and a gallery. Some years were to elapse before the church was consecrated — by Robert Gray, first Bishop of Cape Town.

Soon the development of the town made the church too small for its congregation. About this time, in 1853, the appointment of Grahamstown's first Bishop created the need for a cathedral rather

(Right)
The Anglican Cathedral of St Michael and St George, overlooking the central square of Grahamstown, with the City Hall on the right

(Right)
The ornate baptismal font

than just a parish church, and thought was given to a new building of appropriate size and status.

In terms of the Church Building Act of 1818 — promulgated to celebrate the victorious conclusion of the Napoleonic Wars — the British government allocated a million pounds (later increased by a further half-million) for the building of churches. This led to an upsurge of interest in ecclesiastical architecture in Britain, which, in subsequent decades, became manifest not only in the number of new churches which came into being, but also in the restoration of many older churches, implanting in them more modern features and different styles of construction and decoration.

Popular among architectural styles of that time was the so-called Gothic Revival, with the architect Sir George Gilbert Scott its enthusiastic and dedicated apostle.

It was this well-known English architect who was commissioned to undertake the designing of a cathedral for Grahamstown. He completed the designs for the early stages of the building, notably the soaring bell tower and spire, while, after his death, his son — a prominent architect also named George Gilbert — completed the design work. His share is to be seen in the chancel and the nave, added much later — in 1893 and 1912 respectively and, finally, the Lady Chapel, which was added in 1952.

The noble pillars on either side of the nave are of black Belgian marble, their bases of sandstone

(Left)
The marble memorial to Colonel John Graham, after whom Grahamstown is named

(Below)
The fine carved pulpit, designed by George Gilbert Scott the younger

from Bathurst not far away. The heavy roof beams above the chancel are of teak imported specially from Burma.

The wooden rood screen and the pulpit, both exquisitely carved, were likewise designed by the younger Scott, while the brass lectern is a replica of that designed by his father for Durham Cathedral.

The bells, said to be the heaviest and the first full ring of eight bells on the continent of Africa, were cast in London and installed in the tall tower in 1878.

The dedication of the cathedral to two saints — Michael and George — highlights a serious and historical domestic wrangle between Bishop Webb, appointed to Grahamstown, and Frederick Williams, the Dean, who excluded the newly appointed bishop from St George's Cathedral! The contretemps was taken to the high court — and, indeed, even to the Privy Council in Britain. When the Dean's claim was upheld, the Bishop set up his Throne elsewhere in Grahamstown and designated that building the Pro-Cathedral of St Michael's. On the death of Dean Williams and after reconciliation with the officials of the cathedral, Bishop Webb took possession of St George's where the consecration of the younger Scott's chancel in 1893 provided an opportunity to make manifest the healing of the breach between the two factions and the cathedral was dedicated to both St Michael and St George.

The Holy Trinity Church
Belvidere

(Below)
The pulpit, carved from a single block of sandstone

The setting and architectural proportions of the Anglican Church of the Holy Trinity at Belvidere, in the midst of mouldering graves under the splendid old oaks near the south-western edge of Knysna's lagoon, give it a visual charm and beauty which, with deeper study, are reinforced by its historical interest. Little wonder that this place of worship is so popular with passers-by who throng to admire its manifold attractions.

Construction was based on a design by William Butterfield, Britain's leading architect of the middle and latter nineteenth century, who had made some of his church plans available to Sophy Gray, wife of the first Bishop of Cape Town, for use in South Africa.

The property on which the church was built was owned by Thomas Henry Duthie, a Scottish army officer at the Cape who had visited Knysna on a hunting trip and who later married the daughter of the legendary George Rex from whom he purchased the farm, Belvidere. His wish to build a small church there was strengthened by the visit of Robert Gray, Bishop of Cape Town, who with his wife Sophy was looking at places for new churches to serve the developing Anglican congregations in parts of his far-flung diocese.

With her Sophy Gray carried a portfolio of architect's plans, one of which she selected for a church on the Duthie property. Norman in style, it was modified in size to suit the requirements of the local congregation.

The region happened to be richly endowed with most of the basic building materials. There was yellowwood and stinkwood in abundance and on his farm Duthie had stone for building. Funds were raised in England by Duthie's brother, himself a churchman.

The clean lines of the stone work in this church — to be seen especially in the moulding of the arches of the door and around the windows above it, as well as of the columns between the nave and the chancel — are the work of skilled Scottish masons recruited from a passing immigrant ship. The beauty and the proportions of the magnificent pulpit, hollowed out and carved from a giant block of local sandstone and built into the wall, demonstrate the measure of their dedicated craftsmanship and skill.

Building took some years, but eventually in October 1855 the Holy Trinity Church at Belvidere was consecrated by Bishop Gray.

The bell above the main entrance was cast in England. In the process of being landed at Knysna, it was accidentally dropped overboard and for some while lay at the bottom of the lagoon until it was recovered and eventually set in place.

Through the years, the beauty of this church has been enhanced by the addition of several fine stained-glass windows executed in classical style, memorials to members of the Duthie family, some of whom are buried in the graveyard there. On the south wall a window, designed and made by Charles Groves, ARCA, who taught at the Michaelis School of Fine Art at the University of Cape Town, is a memorial to the two Duthie brothers — William Henry and Alfred George. On the opposite wall a window is dedicated to the memory of Dr Vera Duthie, a botanist. This was designed by Mary Groves, daughter of Charles, who later also taught art at that university.

But it is perhaps the rose window high in the west wall which attracts most interest today. Created by Charles Groves, it is unique in that it is made from fragments of the coloured glass of windows of churches in Britain destroyed by enemy bombing in World War II.

Historical connections with the founders of Knysna and Bishop Gray and his wife, Sophy, as well as with one of England's finest architects, make the Holy Trinity Church at Belvidere one of South Africa's most interesting ecclesiastical buildings. To that interest is added the beauty of its proportions and the romance of its setting.

(Left)
The bell tower above the main entrance

The Sheikh Yusuf Kramat
Faure

Though for more than 150 years after Jan van Riebeeck's arrival at the Cape, the laws imposed by the Dutch East India Company allowed the practice only of the Protestant religion, there were certainly people who quietly practised other faiths, among them a number of Asians. Indeed, the first marriage conducted by Van Riebeeck at the Cape was between a Dutch member of his party and an Indian girl, presumably a Christian Asian. Records do not indicate, however, whether the Asians at the Cape were Hindus or Moslems.

Conscious of the prudence of having personnel to protect the fledgling settlement against marauding Hottentots, Van Riebeeck requested that workers be sent to the Cape from Amboina in Indonesia, men who would provide labour as well protection.

In 1657, to regularise their position at the Cape within the prevailing situation, shortly before the arrival of these Moslem foreigners, the Company saw fit to re-issue a *Placaat* originally promulgated in Amboina 15 years earlier. It allowed Moslems to practise their faith in private without interference. Worship in public remained forbidden, however, and, of course, with worship confined to houses and homes, no mosques were built. At the same time, the *Placaat* forbade the conversion of others — Christians or heathens — to Mohammedanism but did allow Moslems to become Christians.

Moslems other than slaves were also brought to the Cape by the Dutch. Captured militant leaders of uprisings in Amboina were banished to the Cape — away from where they might continue to be a political threat to the authorities.

(Below)
The Sheikh Yusuf Kramat is situated on a hillock which looks across to the mountains near Stellenbosch

(Above)
The text of the plaque incorporated into the memorial minaret

(Left)
Well-worn stone steps lead to the Sheikh's Kramat and monuments, including a tall minaret erected in 1925 as a memorial to Sheikh Yusuf

Among those who arrived in 1694 at the Cape in such circumstances was Sheikh Yusuf who, with his entourage, was persuaded to live in isolation at Zandvliet (now named Faure), some distance from the Castle.

Born in 1626 of noble blood, he was the brother of the Sultan of Macassar who ruled over the little state of Gowa. His status was further enhanced when, after a pilgrimage to Mecca, he attained high religious office and travelled widely, spreading the Islamic faith. In the course of such a crusade to Java he married the daughter of the Sultan of Bantam. Loyally supporting his father-in-law against militant revolutionary forces assisted by the Dutch eager to crush the Sultan's powers, Yusuf was compelled to surrender with his forces and was imprisoned, first in Batavia, then in Ceylon. Fearing the consequences of his influence in the event of his escaping — or being snatched from prison — the authorities sent him yet further away from the focus of possible trouble — to the Cape, out of reach.

His death in May 1699, five years after his arrival, cut short his time there, but during those years at Zandvliet on the shores of False Bay, that Moslem settlement provided refuge for runaway slaves and led to the establishment of what has been described as "the first cohesive Muslim community in South Africa."

In 1862 — long after freedom of worship had been decreed — Moslems at the Cape purchased the Faure Kramat Camping Ground where Yusuf had lived, and there set about erecting a shrine to him. It was built on a hill where he is said to have dreamed he would be buried. The shrine — a *kramat* — rebuilt in 1927, continues to be visited by great numbers of religious pilgrims.

But whether Sheikh Yusuf was in fact interred there is open to considerable doubt. It is claimed in the East that he is buried in Macassar, his birthplace, where there is a similar memorial to this noble leader. There is much to support the contention that the shrine at Faure was developed as a political manoeuvre in a quarrel which threatened to split the Moslem community at the Cape in the latter years of the nineteenth century.

Be that as it may, Sheikh Yusuf has a deserved place in the history of South Africa's multi-cultural development; and the tomb at Faure is a fitting acknowledgement of that contribution.

The shrine is a small green-domed mosque set on a hillock with a sweeping view across the broad flats to the magnificent mountains around Stellenbosch. Passing the old cottage of the custodian at the base and climbing the long flight of rough stone steps to the top, between the overhanging trees which shade the stairway, one sees the memorial minaret. Around the low stone parapet encircling the mosque are several ancient muzzle-loading cannons which look as if they were taken from some eighteenth century man-of-war. Within the shrine a bed is kept covered with rich, ornamented quilts where the spirit of the sleeping Sheikh Yusuf is believed peacefully to reside.

*(Right)
An old muzzle-loading cannon overlooks the stairway from behind the low wall enclosing the grounds of the shrine*

The Synagogue
Kimberley

(Facing page) The interior of the synagogue, looking towards the ornamental apse containing the Ark of the Law

The central synagogue in Kimberley is situated in a quiet suburb of the city, on a corner of the broad, tree-lined Memorial Road and (appropriately) Synagogue Street. An impressive building of brick and stone, it possesses a quiet dignity of its own, while its dominant high dome gives authority to its presence.

Of this Jewish place of worship it has been said that "While by no means one of the largest Synagogues in the country, it is certainly one of the most beautiful." Few would disagree.

Jews in many parts of the world have traditionally played a prominent role in the diamond industry and it is not surprising that numbers of Jewish people were among those quickly attracted by the discovery of the enormously rich diamond fields at Kimberley in 1869. They came from many lands, from all corners of the world; not only merchants and dealers in precious stones, but also workers in other fields. The names of many of them are well known, woven inextricably into the fabric of South Africa's history. Their links with Kimberley lie deep in the roots both of the city and its glittering and romantic prosperity.

It was not long before steps were taken to form a Jewish congregation in the evolving mining town and, in 1871, the Griqualand West Hebrew Association came into being.

For several years the congregation was without a rabbi or synagogue of its own, and was forced to rely on visiting ministers. Only in 1873 did it gain its first full-time minister — the Reverend Berthold Albu — and the congregation set about

building its own place of worship. The foundation stone was laid in 1875 and the building, a "rather unpretentious, galvanised iron structure", was consecrated the following year.

It held 250 worshippers and, with the Jewish community in Kimberley numbering some 1 400 persons, was quickly found to be inadequate.

The De Beers Diamond Company, wishing to own that ground, offered the congregation property in Memorial Road in exchange for the synagogue site. The offer was accepted and the foundation stone of the new building was laid in 1901 and the present synagogue was consecrated by the Reverend Harry Isaacs in September 1902.

A memorial statue of Cecil Rhodes now occupies the site of the earlier building.

The interior is quietly impressive, much of its style reflecting the era of its construction. The stepped women's gallery is supported by tall cast-iron metal poles; the windows all around have small panes of blue, grey and light corn-yellow, bordered by panels of light and dark gold. The arched tops are decorated with floral and patterned motifs in dark blues and yellows. The pews are of imported wood, beautifully grained.

The high-domed ceiling, plastered in panels, follows the curve of the domed exterior. The Ark of the Law is described as "a glorious marbled architectural fantasy of pillars, minarets and domes presenting an Eastern atmosphere". An inscribed marble scroll graces the peak of the arch.

A dark crimson velvet curtain, embroidered with metal thread and worked with decorative jewels, covers the Ark, securely locked away together with a magnificent collection of Torahs — memorial gifts — and fine silver.

Among this synagogue's unique treasures — and appropriate to the world's richest diamond producing area in the world — is its silver Torah-pointer with a diamond at its tip.

(Right) The silver Torah-pointer with a diamond tip — appropriate to Kimberley

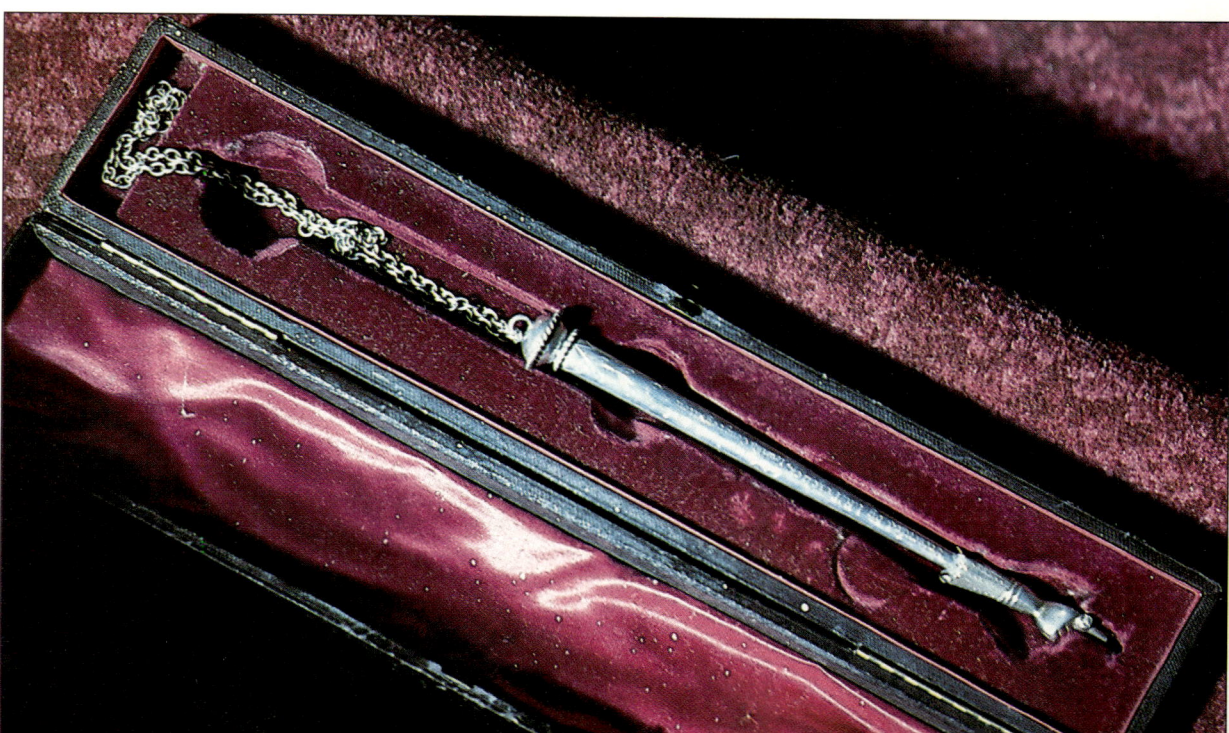

The Moravian Mission
Mamre

(Below)
The Mission Church, dating from 1818, is the fifth oldest extant place of worship in South Africa

(Above) The old water-wheel, which used to grind wheat at the mission

Perhaps it was more pressing matters which, in practice, relegated the organisation of formal education to a lower priority in the early decades of European settlement at the Cape. Perhaps the paucity of pupils was a factor. Such elementary schools as there were were run by the church — which in turn itself was under the control of the Administration. In those years most children were educated at home.

In the hope of speeding the adoption of Christianity by the indigenous people, regulations had been introduced in 1685 stipulating that children of Hottentots adapting to European ways were to be admitted to schools together with the children of settlers and slaves. But, on the whole, efforts at providing schooling on a broad basis made very little headway at the Cape in those early decades. In 1714 a school in Latin and High Dutch set up in Cape Town soon closed when it received little or no public support. But, as far as the Hottentots were concerned, it was the growing wave of missionary zeal in Europe and England at that time which led to the involvement of other church movements in the education of black people in southern Africa.

To the Cape the Moravian Brethren sent George Schmidt, who in 1737 set up a mission station at Baviaan's Kloof. Though this was done with the permission of the authorities, the move was resented both by the farmers of the area and the Dutch Reformed Church.

When Schmidt, not a member of the Dutch Reformed Church, baptised a number of Hottentots, the Council of Policy intervened and officially warned him not to do so again. Disappointed by the immense difficulties he encountered in trying to work with the Hottentots, Schmidt found the intractability of the authorities to be the last straw, and, after seven frustrating years, he returned to Germany.

It was not until 1792 that the Moravians re-opened the mission station, which they named Genadendal, and, in resuming work there, placed considerable emphasis upon training the Hottentots in a number of practical and useful trades as well as upon religious instruction, of course, and the usual school subjects.

Their success led them to open further missions — a step encouraged by the British authorities who, in 1806, had again taken control of the Cape. The first of these new missions was at Groen Kloof, where, from 1701 to 1791, there had been a military outpost set up to protect a farming concession producing meat for the Dutch East India Company in that lush, well-watered country. In due course the missionaries named it Mamre, after the place where, according to the Book of Genesis, Abram had taken his tent and settled.

The original façade of the church, built there in 1818, was designed by John Melvill, a government official, but its classical English style was severely altered by the baroque style of the gables added later. Its roof is still thatched, adding mellowness to its appearance and the romance of its history. The interior is plain and painted throughout in white. The church remains the fifth oldest place of worship in South Africa.

The mission, with its venerable oaks and white-washed cottages set in gaily coloured gardens, is situated a little way from the village itself, a preserve of Cape Coloured people only.

In 1830 a mill was built to grind wheat grown there by the community. At first it was a horse mill, but after some years this form of power was replaced by a large water-wheel which, in turn, gave way to steam power. Later it was driven by a diesel-engine. Today the wheat is ground elsewhere, but the old mill, recently restored, stands as a reminder of Mamre's past and of the mission's contribution to the nation's heritage.

(Facing page) Since the church building is often unable to accommodate all who wish to attend services, proceedings are relayed by loud-speaker to those of the congregation outside — for whose convenience this collection box is placed

Mission Church of the Holy Cross
Mackay's Nek

(Above) The mission church below the mountain buttresses

Mackay's Nek, people will tell you, is between Queenstown and Lady Frere in the Transkei, a short distance from the border.

The architecture and ornamentation of the little Catholic country church there is essentially African in character.

Standing below the sheltering crest of a low hill and overlooked by tall mountains behind, the church gazes across the wide plain of a grassy basin peppered here and there with isolated clusters of huts and random dwellings. To the south-east, on the hilltops high above the church, is an unusual cluster of bulbous, rocky outcrops which cling centrally together to form a single dramatic feature like some gigantic prehistoric trefoiled monument.

This unusual formation provided the missionaries with the idea for the shape of the church they were intent on creating near its base: large rondavels centrally linked in clover fashion which roughly reiterates the upper shape of that mountain watching over the region.

With the help of members of the mission they designed and built this place of worship. Sister Pientia Selhorst, a talented artist and nun of the religious Order of Sisters of the Precious Blood, came from Mariannhill (q.v.) near Durban to decorate the new church.

The largest of the rondavels houses a sanctuary dominated by a magnificent, large mosaic of Christ in sombre greys and blues with the Cross outlined in gold. The altar, in the centre of the raised circular sanctuary, is a heavy stone entablature resting on two large, squared supporting rocks. Wrought-iron railings separate the sanctuary from the circular ambulatory which on each side of the altar ends with abutting walls also decorated with fine mosaic frescoes.

This main rondavel is heightened by a drum supported internally on six substantial pillars and itself supports the conical roof. Clerestory windows of clear glass around the drum admit the bright African light, illuminating this central liturgical area amid the softer light of the rest of the interior where nature's light is diffused by the colours of the stained-glass windows.

On either side is a smaller rondavel, each open to the altar and the sanctuary, thus forming smaller chapels.

The fourth rondavel is similarly open to the sanctuary and forms a continuous part of the nave, while at its rear a small separated area around the entrance may be regarded as the porch.

Plain pine benches provide seating.

Construction is of local stone, some of it roughly dressed, some water-worn and smooth. The upper

(Left)
The Crucifixion — a large mosaic in the sanctuary, created by Sister Pientia Selhorst

(Below)
A plan of the Mission Church of the Holy Cross

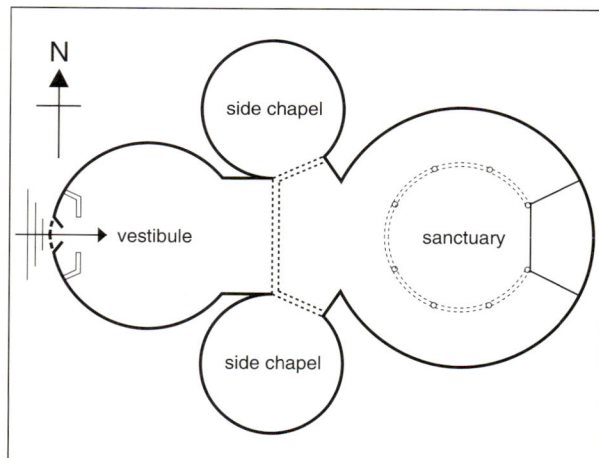

parts of the walls, both inside and out, are plastered, the separation of the plain stone base from the white-painted upper section being delineated by a decorative frieze of African patterns. The floors are of slasto and the ceilings of white boards. The corrugated iron roofs are painted silver, their dazzling shine seen from afar and, on a sunny day, are blinding to the gaze from close by.

A band of geometrical African motifs decorates parts of the dun-coloured exterior, as well as the parts of the drum above the sanctuary. Over the entrance a painted stylised Cross is flanked by a prominent Alpha and Omega, facing west across the broad grassy veld. This is the work of two young Zulu artists sent especially to assist with the decoration of this church at the time of its construction in 1959.

The interest created by the unusual shape and structure is further enhanced by the fine decorative art work created by Sister Pientia and executed under her supervision. Apart from the impressive mosaics in the sanctuary are her moving Stations of the Cross on wooden panels in the vestibule and linked by a patterned frieze painted by Rosina Qwalana.

The belfry is no conventional tower, tall or otherwise. Three bells, painted silver, hang from a low beam, within reach even of a child, and are protected from the weather by a strip of roofing. Separate from the church building itself the belfry is enclosed by rows of indigenous aloes. The perimeter of the whole church complex is fenced — not to separate the church from its people, but rather to keep out stray beasts. Any adverse impact the enclosing wire may have is softened by rows of tall aloes which, in turn, add immensely to the African character of this attractive Catholic country church.

Nederduitse Gereformeerde Kerk
Cradock

The classical splendour of the present Dutch Reformed Church in the eastern Cape town of Cradock is emphasised by its commanding position on a small hill which gives it a fine and unimpeded view over the town. Well sited, it sees — and is seen.

Cradock was born in travail, created originally as a defence post for the protection of the settlers against marauding Xhosas from across the colonial border early in the nineteenth century. It was named after Sir John Cradock, then Governor of the Cape.

John Evans of the London Missionary Society, Cradock's first minister, arrived at the Cape in 1815 and, prior to coming to Cradock, had been engaged in missionary duties in Bechuanaland. Interestingly, his appointment in the middle of 1817 pre-dated the formal establishment of a diocese at Cradock which, as a consequence of bureaucratic delays, came into being officially only in June 1818. Consequently there was no established church building when he arrived. Services were conducted at the minister's house, while *Nagmaal* was celebrated quarterly under a tarpaulin slung between two wagons in the garden of the parsonage. A traveller relates how, in 1822, between 300 and 450 wagons used to congregate in the village on such occasions.

Funds were raised, however, and building began on ground purchased for the purpose. Stone was quarried locally and brought by wagon to the site. Construction was completed towards the end

of 1823, a squat cruciform church with a gabled front which John Evans did not live to see. He died suddenly earlier that year at a young age and John Taylor, a Scots minister, took his place.

Memorial plaques to these two first ministers are to be seen — simple and elegant — on the rear wall of the present church.

That first church served the congregation for almost 40 years until the increased number of worshippers had outstripped its capacity. In April 1862 the congregation voted in favour of erecting a new church on the site of the old. A temporary place of worship was built for interim use and a campaign was initiated to raise the necessary

(Above left)
The interior, showing the organ and the magnificent pulpit

(Above right)
Detail of the carved pulpit

money for both the new and the temporary churches.

An advertisement calling for plans for a new stone church brought no less than 16 replies. The first prize of 30 pounds went to the Cape Town architects, Welchman and Read.

Work begun in December 1863 did not always proceed smoothly through the ensuing years and progress was not without a number of interruptions. But by September 1868 the building was complete, the pews were in place and an expert from Port Elizabeth was busy refurbishing and installing the organ taken from the older church.

Visitors thronged to Cradock for the inauguration. Excitement ran high and the town was *en fête* for this important occasion.

Plans decreed that all should rendezvous at the temporary church at 9 a.m. and that, after a short ceremony there, people would proceed in procession to Cradock's new place of worship for its consecration and the service of dedication.

The crowd duly assembled, but soon became restive when nothing happened. The more impatient went home; others, similarly impatient, hung about anxiously waiting for the ceremony to begin. After a while the reason for the delay became known.

The building contractor, who must have been aware that funds were insufficient to cover full costs, refused to hand over the keys of the building until he was guaranteed payment. At the temporary church while the minister was doing his best to assuage the growing impatience of the waiting crowd with a sermon and hymns, behind the scenes the building committee was trying to reason with the contractor. The impasse was solved only when a number of citizens gave the assurances he demanded and visitors were able to proceed to the new church. There it was found that the numbers were too great to be accommodated inside the church and further confusion reigned.

Architecturally this church is most attractive, its sturdy proportions emphasising its importance to the community. A visitor to Cradock during its construction, seeing the work in progress, felt assured that this church would be "the most durable building in the Colony."

Inside is a fine wooden pulpit. The first six rows of pews form an arc facing the pulpit, while the rest are set straight and parallel respectively with the pulpit.

Above the large rectangular windows with their panels of green, white and pale gold are small roundels with rosettes of star-shaped coloured glass.

The organ, with its silvered pipes, is situated behind the pulpit, while the spacious gallery at the back is supported by slender, fluted metal columns with gold-painted acanthus capitals. The overall effect is light and elegant.

Welchman and Read, the architects, based their plans on the design of the well-known church of St Martin-in-the-Fields which stands adjacent to the South African Embassy in Trafalgar Square in London. Consecrated in 1726, St Martin-in-the-Fields became much admired for its Palladian style and grandeur. Flattered, the architect, James Gibb, a pupil of Sir Christopher Wren, published drawings of the building for the use and study of any who wished to build a similar church.

The Corinthian portico and triangular pediment, the solid pillars and tall Gothic, tapered steeple and clock are features common to each of these places of worship.

The history of Cradock's Dutch Reformed Church epitomises the close links between South Africa and the United Kingdom. Set in a town named after a British Governor and with its first minister a Welshman and its second a Scot, its architecture essentially English, this impressive building sets the seal upon those historic founding links.

The Yellowwood Church of St Andrew
Redbourne

Universally, wooden churches are not rare. Many are to be seen in Scandinavia and, too, in small towns and villages of North America. Nature has endowed those regions with plentiful supplies of suitable timber which for centuries has been used in the construction of buildings, both domestic and ecclesiastical.

England claims to have the oldest wooden church in the world. St Andrew's in Essex was built in the year 845 — on the site of a previous church which is reputed to have been a Celtic, pre-Christian place of worship. It has been skilfully built of oak, with holes bored through its stout walls for ventilation.

But, doubtless on account of the climate and other local predators of timber — as well as the paucity of its availability — wood has been used very seldom as a primary material for building in South Africa. In this country there are, however, two small wooden churches — not of stout oak, but both of indigenous yellowwood, equally hard and durable.

One is at Bulwer in the midlands of Natal (q.v.). The other — St Andrew's — is at Redbourne near

(Above)
Old graves lie in peace in the quiet valley beside the Yellowwood church of St Andrew at Redbourne

(Facing page)
The intruding bush restlessly seeks to reclaim its domain

(Above left) The heavy wooden door protects the inside of the church from stray animals

(Above right) The plaster of the interior conceals the timber of the walls

Plettenberg Bay. Both were built by early settlers and both are dedicated to the Anglican faith.

St Andrew's church in the Cape was built by William Newdigate who had married a daughter of the Duthies of Belvidere and who owned the farm Buccleigh near Plettenberg Bay. He built it for use by the people of the area, logging the yellowwood from his own property. Traces of confetti at the church door confirm that it is still used today, worshippers from the district coming — when services are held — from the Piesang Valley along the narrow, overgrown, rough road which, flanked by trees and leafy bushes, dwindles into a country lane as it nears the little chapel.

Building was completed in 1851 but the church was consecrated only in 1855 when Bishop Gray visited the region — on which tour of this sector of his diocese he also consecrated the beautiful Holy Trinity Church at Belvidere (q.v.).

The roof is of corrugated iron and the simple, plain interior of the church (unlike that at Bulwer) is plastered. The heavy wooden door has large ornamental wrought-iron hinges and is watched over by a tall, hooded bell-tower of timber beams close by.

The church stands in one corner of a large, sloping grassy space enclosed by heavy bush which never ceases in its efforts to thrust into the clearing to reclaim its ancient domain. Through the passing years graves on the verge of the clearing have become victims of its python-like possessiveness.

Some men die peacefully, soon quietly forgotten; others die in battle, their fame scarcely more lasting. In the endless universal pageant of nature, sooner or later, the grass enshrouds them all.

As Carl Sandburg has told us,

I am the grass; I cover all . . .
. . . I am the grass,
Let me work.

On the crumbling gravestones, dotted here and there in no discernible order, those dates still legible cover many decades and several generations, a rustic microcosm of local history, now being forgotten.

They lie in silence, those graves, isolated and undisturbed amid the beauty of the surrounding hills and in the infinite hush of the bush, accepting with careless equanimity the endless parade of passing days and the continuing chain of sunshine and rain.

The Rhenish Church
Stellenbosch

As interesting as the history of this beautiful little church undoubtedly is and as fascinating as its architecture may be, few will dispute that it is the splendour of its setting which really gives this — one of the oldest mission churches in South Africa — much of its charm and its special appeal.

Set on the southern edge of the Braak, the grassy open space in the town's centre, this Rhenish Church with its gleaming white-gabled front edged sharply against the majestic, rugged purple-blue Groot Drakenstein mountains, looks across the greenness at its cousin, the Anglican church of St Mary's, on the north side of the Braak.

The history of the present church began with the founding, in 1801, of a branch of the South African Christian Missionary Society in Stellenbosch, primarily for the purpose of educating slaves. The success of the Society and the increase in the numbers of its members made it impossible to continue its activities in private homes.

A decision to build a church became a reality when ground at the southern end of the Braak was presented to the mission by the Stellenbosch Turf Club. The small church built there was consecrated early in 1824.

Soon, however, this became too small and the building had to be enlarged. Further growth in the size of the congregation made it necessary to extend the building yet again and the north wing was added. The bigger building was inaugurated in 1840 — as the date on the gable still tells. In that same year the church was taken over by the Rhenish Missionary Society which administered it until 1944 when the Dutch Reformed Missionary Society assumed responsibility for its activities, though it still remains known as the Rhenish Church.

(Above)
The Rhenish Church on the Braak stands against the magnificent background of the mountains

(Above) The date on the gable indicates the year of the church's inauguration. The belfry was designed later by Blersch

The building is T-shaped, the bar of the T being the original construction, while the additions are represented by the stem which reaches out towards the Braak.

The baroque belfry on the western side, with its twin bells, designed by Blersch, the Town Clerk of Stellenbosch, matches the gracious style of the main church building, belying the fact that it was added many years later — indeed, only well into the twentieth century.

The origin of the magnificent, ornate pulpit adds an interesting paragraph to the long history of this place of worship.

When the church was first built, funds could not be stretched for the acquisition of a pulpit. Not long before, however, the Groote Kerk in Cape Town had replaced its older pulpit by a magnificent new and very ornate work of art, carved by Anton Anreith, which today is still the pride of that church (q.v.). The Rhenish Church asked the

(Above)
This fine ornamental pulpit was created by Simon Pieter Christoffel Londt, a Cape Town craftsman, in 1853 and acquired by the Rhenish Church 10 years later

Groote Kerk for the use of the pulpit no longer needed in Cape Town. The request was granted and the pulpit, installed in the Rhenish Church, was used there for a number of years.

In 1852 the Dutch Reformed Church in Stellenbosch replaced its pulpit with a new one made by a craftsman named Londt in Cape Town. This served the Moederkerk well for about 10 years until it was felt that Londt's pulpit — which, though beautiful, was rather squat — did not match the soaring Gothic lines of Stellenbosch's fine new place of worship. The construction of a new and more appropriate pulpit was commissioned.

Londt's fine pulpit and the matching lectern were then donated to the Rhenish Church where they took the place of the old pulpit from the Groote Kerk in Cape Town. Their stylish elegance has added a note of opulence to the simplicity of the interior of this beautiful and historic church.

St Patrick on the Hill
Hogsback

(Above) The interior of the little rondavel chapel at Hogsback

Among the several small places of worship in South Africa, the little chapel of St Patrick on the Hill at Hogsback in the heart of the Amatola Mountains in the eastern Cape is one of the smallest. The building consists of a single rondavel of ordinary size built of locally quarried stone. No pretentiously decorated doors grace its simple entrance, nor are its two ordinary domestic windows adorned by any extravagantly coloured emblems and designs. Its roof is of simple thatch, low and conical, the top crowned by a humble wooden Cross reaching to heaven as devoutly as the tall soaring ornamented steeple of any great urban cathedral.

No chiming clock here disturbs the rustic tranquillity with noisy proclamations of the

*(Left)
The original little church, set under an old oak, with the sundial on the right*

incessant march of the hours. A simple sundial, set on a slender stone plinth on the paved forecourt of the little church, on sunny days silently discloses the hour to those for whom time is important and who are impatient to know.

Alongside a quiet country road and set about with gardens and bushy rhododendrons, the tiny church is guarded by a noble and mature oak whose protective outspread branches in summer provide shade against the sun's heat and, in winter, help to deflect the snows from its conical thatched roof.

Through the bushes and rhododendrons beneath the oak, one catches glimpses of rolling country hills and vast valleys, glory piled upon glory across the vast African landscape.

The simplicity of the church's construction is echoed in the interior. The altar is of stone. The pews, close together, are of plain pine. The division between the cramped nave and the chancel is also marked out in stone. A draped hanging on the front wall gives emphasis to the silver Cross which presides over the altar.

A metal plate near the altar invites worshippers and visitors to remember those whose inspiration made this place.

The plaque reads, simply:

> Remember
> Cherrie and Kenneth
> Hobart Houghton
> who in 1935 built
> this Chapel and Garden
> to the Glory of God.

The spirit and the simple beauty of this little building, belonging to the Anglican Church but used by all denominations, finds an echo in a verse set out near the door for all to read:

> Pause ere thou enter,
> Traveller, and bethink thee
> How holy, yet how homelike, is this place:
> Time that thou spendest humbly here shall link thee
> With men unknown who once were of thy race;
> This is thy Father's House; to Him address thee.
> Whom here His children worship face to face:
> He at thy coming in with Peace will bless thee;
> Thy going out make joyful with His grace.

It is its simplicity and the romance of its size which characterise this church of St Patrick and which have come to distinguish it from many other village places of worship in South Africa. Unfortunately that romance has been ravaged by progress and a developing need for a bigger church to serve the growing population. Rather than abandon or demolish the existing church, plans have been drawn for extensions to the building.

The extensions — it has been promised — will faithfully follow the style and character of the original building which, its interior unchanged, will become a part of the enlarged church. The sundial will be moved and reset: the guardian oak tree will remain for as long as nature allows.

No longer will St Patrick on the Hill then be one of South Africa's smallest churches. Hopefully, however, its character, enchantment and romance will abide as part of the history of its origins.

The Myrtle Rigg Church
Bonnievale

(Above) The little Norman-style church that is an unusual memorial to a young girl

On the broad plains against the magnificent backdrop of the Langeberg Mountains in the south-western Cape, in the pleasant little town of Bonnievale, is a small, Norman-style stone church dedicated — unusually — to the memory of a young girl.

The history of this place of worship is a moving and poignant one. Churches are generally dedicated to the founders and saints of the various religions and sometimes to others prominent in the spreading of those faiths. Eminent or heroic men and women are remembered and honoured in places of worship by memorials and statues: brave men killed in battle, explorers and adventurers, doctors and nurses, poets and politicians — all of whom, in many and various ways in their time, contributed to the welfare of people. But a church dedicated to a young child denied by the tenderness of her years from achieving greatness is rare, and indeed the church is reputed to be the only one in the world built in memory of a young girl.

The inscription on a plaque in the sanctuary reads: "To the Glory of God and in loving Memory of Mary Myrtle Rigg who although of tender years was anxious that a church be built."

The church has not been formally named after the little girl, but inevitably in the circumstances it has become known as the Myrtle Rigg Church.

An inscription on her grave in the churchyard describes her as the "only darling child" of Christopher Rigg — the founder and benefactor of Bonnievale — and his wife. Myrtle was an affectionate, happy and loving daughter, seeking always to help those around her and ever eager to go to church. On her deathbed in September 1911 she asked her father to build her a little church.

Christopher Rigg saved money to fulfill the request and on his farm some years later erected this sturdy little stone church next to Myrtle's grave on a low koppie which overlooks Bonnievale. He gave the church property to the Anglican community there.

Entrance to the church is through a large porch, past heavily carved doors from Zanzibar. Large squares of black and white Italian marble make up the chess-board floor, while the barrel-vaulted

*(Left)
The grave of Myrtle Rigg
in the churchyard at
Bonnievale*

ceiling of the nave is attractively roughened by small river pebbles of varying colours.

Inscriptions on a number of memorial plaques on the walls — many to the Rigg family — give emphasis to the poignancy of the church's unusual origins.

Over the entrance to the nave a painting of a little girl amid flowers and bushes bears the Old Testament inscription, "A little child shall lead them" (Isaiah).

A small part of the surrounding graveyard is enclosed by a stone wall that separates the family graves from the others. There Myrtle lies in the shade of tall eucalyptus trees, the hush broken by the soft cooing of doves and the gentle sound of the wind in the leaves. Myrtle's childish signature has been copied on to a marble slab at the foot of the memorial which marks her burial place adjacent to a memorial to her father, who was drowned at sea several years later.

St Luke's: A Private Chapel
Onrus

(Right) The private chapel of St Luke's stands beside the road at Onrus

Among the few small and private churches in South Africa the little Greek-style chapel at Onrus, near Hermanus in the Cape, is certainly one of the most interesting.

It is a modern replica of the type of little churches which abound in the remote villages of rural Greece and on the quaysides of many of the old fishing harbours in the Mediterranean islands; used mainly by sailors and fishermen before they venture out to face the hazards of the sea and, with gratitude for their safe return and the fruits of their successful labours, when the boats come home again.

Small and lime-washed, these minuscule places of worship stand close to the sea, their characteristic white barrel-vaulted roofs and domes bright against the rich blue of the sunlit waters.

While not on the water's edge, the chapel at Onrus stands within sound of the restless surging of the Indian Ocean, though an accompanying view of the sea is inhibited by trees and vegetation, by the undulations in the terrain and, today, by the increasing density of the habitation of what used to be the quiet, isolated domain of a handful of writers and artists seeking solitude in which to work.

(Above)
The small stone altar in the sanctuary

The chapel is the brain-child of two women artists, Maxie Steytler and Tertia Knaap, who, when Onrus was quieter, set up their studios there, the former to spin and weave, the latter to continue with her sculpture, her painting and creative art. Besides their own work, they now conduct art classes in a well-equipped school, close at hand yet screened from the church by thick indigenous bush.

The chapel, dedicated to St Luke, stands on a low, bushy and rocky knoll, with a short zigzag rough-paved stone path leading from the roadway to the heavy double doors of the entrance below a simple Crete-inspired bell tower. Designed in 1985 by Jack van Rensburg, a friend and architect in Pretoria, the church measures 2,5 metres in width and 4,1 metres in length. Among the ecclesiastical ornaments in the small semi-circular apse are a number of fine modern icons painted in classical Byzantine style, and four small *dalles-de-verre* stained-glass windows by Leo Theron which contribute colour to the otherwise unrelieved whiteness of the interior. The minuscule chancel is separated from the nave by sandstone slabs, their plainness relieved by incised decorative crosses. The small, low altar is also of local sandstone.

Traditionally Greek churches have no pews and the congregation stands throughout the services. It cannot thus be said that this chapel "seats" any estimated number of worshippers. The maximum number of standing persons at any one time, however, is thought to be 15. In one corner there is a small bench — "for emergency use".

For all its charm and attractiveness St Luke's church is no mere architectural ornament. And though in style remote in both time and space from the traditions which inspired its concept, this chapel is not just some exotic exhibition piece. It has been conventionally consecrated and is used regularly, not only by its owners, but also by others who similarly find the dignified simplicity of its interior a quiet and peaceful haven for prayer and meditation.

92 The Church of the Vow
    Pietermaritzburg

96 The Roman Catholic Mission
    Mariannhill

100 All Saints Church
    Ladysmith

103 Griqua National Independent Church
    Kokstad

106 Buddhist Retreat Centre
    Ixopo

109 The Yellowwood Chapel of
    the Holy Trinity
    Bulwer

112 The Soofi Mosque
    Ladysmith

115 A Drakensberg Country Church
    Cathkin Peak

117 The Shree Poongavana Amman Temple
    Durban

119 The Church of the Good Shepherd
    Hlabisa

122 The Sri-Sri Radha-Radhanath
    Temple of Understanding
    Durban

125 The Llandaff Oratory
    Van Reenen

127 The Subrahmanya Temple
    Tinley Manor

(Facing page)

"I will lift up mine eyes to the hills..."

*The plain window of the
Drakensburg Country Church, Cathkin Peak,
beautified by nature, needs no further adornment*

Natal

The Church of the Vow
Pietermaritzburg

(Right) The old Church of the Vow is now a museum. The statue in the foreground is that of Gerrit Maritz

"...ons 'n huis tot Sy eer sal oprig..."

Today the graceful whitewashed building in lower Church Street in Pietermaritzburg, venerated as the Church of the Vow, is but the shell of the historic place of worship which once graced that site.

It is no longer a church, nor indeed has it been for some decades. But its spiritual importance remains, wrapped in the fabric of that building. Its architecture is perhaps too plain to evoke admiration on that score; merely a squat rectangular building, though not without some elegance in its simplicity. Devoid now of ecclesiastical ornament, the building is without any soaring spire or traditionally gilded weathercock reaching proudly into the blue of the sky; it has no old, deep-throated church bells to summon worshippers to prayer, nor today do the swelling sounds of an organ within echo thanks

(Left)
The words of the Voortrekker's Vow is set in a plaque in the vestibule of the adjacent modern church

> HIER STAAN ONS
> VOOR DIE HEILIGE GOD VAN HEMEL EN AARDE
> OM 'N GELOFTE AAN HOM TE DOEN, DAT,
> AS HY ONS SAL BESKERM
> EN ONS VYAND IN ONS HAND SAL GEE,
> ONS DIE DAG EN DATUM ELKE JAAR AS 'N DANKDAG,
> SOOS 'N SABBAT SAL DEURBRING,
> EN DAT ONS 'N HUIS TOT SY EER SAL OPRIG
> WAAR DIT HOM BEHAAG,
> EN DAT ONS OOK AAN ONS KINDERS SAL SÊ DAT
> HULLE MET ONS DAARIN MOET DEEL TOT
> NAGEDAGTENIS OOK VIR DIE OPKOMENDE GESLAGTE.
> WANT DIE EER VAN SY NAAM SAL VERHEERLIK WORD
> DEUR DIE ROEM EN DIE EER VAN OORWINNING
> AAN HOM TE GEE.

Statues of Piet Retief (left) and Gerrit Maritz (right) in the forecourt of the Church of the Vow. Their names together form that of Natal's capital, Pietermaritzburg

and praise to God. That is now left to the new, modern church at its side.

But the historical symbolism of this old building is deeply ingrained in Afrikaner culture, entrenched not merely in the nation's history, but also in the very ethos of the people. Built to commemorate the Covenant with God entered into by a handful of Trekkers, the old building, though no longer a place of worship, is an icon representative of faith and of history.

The story is well known. The Voortrekkers, moving into Natal early in the nineteenth century, were repeatedly attacked by the Zulus and, to put an end to the harassment, decided to break the might of Dingaan and his armies. As they approached the Zulu country, near what is now Wasbank, the Trekker commando made a solemn vow that if they were victorious in the impending battle they would observe the day forever as a sabbath and would "found a House in memory of His great name".

It was 5 a.m. on Sunday, 16 December 1838 when the Zulu impis attacked the Voortrekker laager on the banks of a tributary of the Buffalo River — on which, not far away, other mighty and historic battles later came to be fought.

The battle raged until mid-morning when, decisively defeated and broken, the depleted Zulu forces began their retreat, pursued by mounted Voortrekkers. The tributary became known as Blood River, from the colour of its waters after the conflict.

The victory validated the Trekkers' vow, and taking possession of the region, they established the Republic of Natalia and a capital, Pietermaritzburg — named after two of their leaders, Piet Retief and Gerrit Maritz. To honour their pledge to God and, with gratitude for their victory at Blood River, they decided that at that place they would build their memorial church.

Once funds were raised, construction began in April 1840. The church was inaugurated in the following year. As a building it was not a success, however. The flat wooden roof was not proof against rain and was replaced by a pitched roof of thatch with gables at each end.

Within 15 years the building had become too small, making it necessary to replace it with a larger church. This was built close by and consecrated in 1861.

The old building — no longer used as a place of worship — was sold and through the passing years saw service variously as a school, a blacksmith's shop, a mineral water factory, a chemist's shop and a tea-room.

But its ties with history proved implacable and in 1908 Afrikaners decided to preserve the old church in the spirit in which it was founded and built. Money was raised and the building was restored and renovated. On the Day of the Vow in

1912 it was opened as a museum of Voortrekker memorabilia and handed to the South African Government for safe-keeping.

Soon the second church became too small and in turn gave way to a new place of worship which was built on the same site. It was consecrated in 1962, 101 years after its predecessor. The architect was P.R. le Roux of Stellenbosch. A massive modern building, it has large bronze statues of Piet Retief (by Coert Steynberg) and Gerrit Maritz (by Jo Roos) in the forecourt.

Embedded in the wall of the impressive entrance porch are set out, in golden letters, the words of the Covenant entered into by the Voortrekkers on 9 December 1838. This church is the continuing fulfilment of that sacred promise.

Note: *There is another Dutch Reformed Church of the Vow in Louis Trichardt in the northern Transvaal. It was built to fulfil a similar vow made by General Joubert in October 1898 on the eve of battle against the militant Bavenda who were harassing Trekker settlers in the Soutpansberg.*

(Above)
These trees in the church's garden were planted on 16 December 1912 when the renovated memorial church was handed over to the Government

(Left)
The steeple of the modern Church of the Vow

The Roman Catholic Mission
Mariannhill

*(Right)
The towers of
St Joseph's Cathedral
peer over the trees at
Mariannhill*

Set in Natal's verdant, rolling countryside, the Mariannhill Mission near Durban is today a flourishing and dynamic institution that still upholds the traditions of service to the community established more than a century ago.

The mission was founded in 1882 by Father Franz Pfanner, who came to South Africa from Europe with a small band of Trappist monks. New to Africa and ignorant of conditions, they had first been directed to the arid land of the eastern Cape. Devastating drought conditions there led a frustrated Father Pfanner to seek an alternative site on which to establish a mission in South Africa, and the lush green hills of Natal must have presented an attractive alternative.

Perhaps in the lush verdure of the bush and the gentle roll of the Natal hills Father Pfanner saw something of his native Austria, with fields to feed the mission and hillsides to provide timber for building and, if needs be, also to keep the monks warm in the mild winters.

After searching for a suitable site, in December 1882 Father Pfanner acquired ground near Pinetown, not far from Durban. At once the monks began clearing the bush from the hills and valleys for the building of a permanent mission. Trees were felled, bricks were made. One by one, the buildings arose and the monks moved into the new quarters, happily vacating the rough and ready temporary accommodation. At the same time, they set about ploughing the earth and planting seed, and the fertile soil soon responded richly to cultivation.

They dedicated the mission to the Blessed Virgin Mary and her mother, Saint Anne. Father Pfanner named it Mariannhill and that name has endured and its reputation has spread.

Development continued at a remarkable pace. Within two years buildings included a chapel and living quarters for the monks as well as workshops, storerooms, stables and cattle kraals, besides a sick-bay, a bakery and a small guest cottage. Father Franz, the Prior, lived simply in a small wood-and-iron shack close by, its Spartan simplicity reflecting the dedication, humility and character of this great man.

Among the monks were a number of craftsmen, one of whom was an engineer of outstanding ability, Brother Nivard. It was he who surveyed the land and planned developments, laying out roads and designing bridges on the new property. His reputation soon spread beyond the confines of the monastery and his expertise was used by the South African Railways — who rewarded him with a free rail pass.

News of the mission's success spread quickly and from Europe attracted numbers to the Trappist ranks at Mariannhill where their labours added further impetus to its rapid development. The Umhlatuzana River was dammed and water piped both to the mission and to the farm. By 1884 water from the river was being used to power a sawmill.

The foundations of the mission now solidly laid, Father Pfanner turned to developing other aspects of his missionary work.

With a doctor among the monks, it was possible to extend the health services to the sick outside the mission and accommodation was built to house such patients. Schoolhouses were erected and in 1884 boarding facilities were made available to boys of all creeds and all nationalities. The mixing of blacks and whites in this fashion evoked criticism among the colonists. Father Pfanner remained undeterred, however. He realised that a start had to be made to develop Christianity among the black peoples and to wean the Africans from their traditional beliefs and customs. The place to begin, he averred, was with the children. That the task would not be easy nor results quickly achieved, he well appreciated.

The following year saw the arrival at Mariannhill of five young German women who, in response to Father Pfanner's appeals, had volunteered to tackle the education of African girls and to provide them with vocational training as nurses, teachers and mothers.

Their ranks were soon swelled by further recruits. At Father Pfanner's instigation, these nuns became the founder members of an Order known as the Missionary Sisters of the Precious Blood.

(Above left)
A magnificent wooden carving of Mary and Jesus above the altar in the chapel at Mariannhill monastery

(Above)
Memorial statue of Father Pfanner above his grave at Mariannhill, the mission he founded

(Right)
St Joseph's Cathedral

Development was not limited to Mariannhill, however. By 1888 Father Pfanner had founded no less than nine associate missions in various parts of Natal. This growth was made possible not least by the ready flow of men and women — mostly German — who were attracted to the Trappist calling at Mariannhill. By 1890 there were no less than 200 monks and 127 Sisters working there and at its associated missions. By 1898 Mariannhill had become the largest abbey in the world in terms of people involved in its operations as well as in respect of the territory it covered.

In recognition of the hard work which had built up Mariannhill, the monastery had become an abbey and Father Pfanner became its first abbot. The honour of the promotion in no way altered his rigorous mode of living. With ingrained humility, he continued his simple life and the little corrugated-iron hut, plain and unadorned, in which he dwelt, became known as the "smallest abbey in the world".

All was not plain sailing, however. In a sense his success and the achievements of the mission led to an increase in the difficulties they had to face, within their own Brotherhood as well as among the public — both black and white — of Natal.

Zulu chiefs began to view the expansion of the mission's activities as a threat to their rule and their ownership of land and, too, saw the increasing hold of the monks over their subjects as a threat to their tribal authority. At the same time, the colonists grew worried by the mission's acceptance of blacks and whites on a basis of equality, without discrimination of colour and race.

As if these problems were not enough, suddenly from within the Order there came a number of

unbelievably hostile accusations against Abbot Pfanner, prompted perhaps by jealousy at the unique success of his mission. Charges relating to his administration of Mariannhill led to his suspension until investigations had proved the allegations unfounded. Two years later he was accused of breaching certain rules of the Trappist Order and of practices forbidden in the Order: he had permitted novices to work outside the confines of the monastery; and, without permission of the Order, he had sometimes relaxed the rule of silence and the rules of dress.

The charges were not disputed. Judgement took little or no account, however, of the impossibility of applying strictly monastic regulations to missionary work in a diversified society and among primitive peoples. No allowance was made for adapting to tropical conditions dress designed for the climate of Europe. Nor did the merits of his achievements seem to influence the judgement.

Condemnation was harsh. The abbot was suspended, and forbidden to communicate with Brothers or Sisters at any of the missions he had founded. He was ordered to leave Mariannhill. It was a bitter blow which he accepted with humility and without question or hostility.

Franz Pfanner spent the first year of his suspension in prayer and lonely contemplation, and then, in April 1894, founded a mission in the Drakensberg which he called Emmaus. There he laboured and the mission prospered. It was at Emmaus that, at the age of 84 and still in Christian service, he died. He was buried at Mariannhill — the place he founded and loved. A memorial statue watches over his grave.

Sadly, he did not live to see, in the year of his death, the separation by papal decree of the monastery and the Mariannhill mission from the Trappist Order — to enable the missionary work to be tackled unfettered by the canonical rules which he was accused of breaching. Too late he was vindicated.

Today Mariannhill is larger and more influential than ever. Its diocese embraces more than a quarter of a million Catholic adherents. The large monastery has a fine church, built by the monks and with a magnificently carved altar. The twin towers of St Joseph's Cathedral peer across the tops of the trees lining the avenues of the rambling settlement. Below the small rotunda chapel, built in 1919, is the Convent of the Missionary Sisters of the Precious Blood. Within the mission are no less than 12 chapels. St Francis College educates African boys and girls. The up-to-date hospital of St Mary serves all races. There is a retreat house and an old age home. Trades at Mariannhill include a printing works and a publishing house, a metalwork and engineering shop and cabinet-making departments. A tailor's shop makes canonical robes and outfits for other institutions. Agriculture is another of the many practical subjects taught there.

It was here, in more recent years, that Sister Pientia Selhorst, a gifted artist, had her studio in which she designed the magnificent stained-glass windows, mosaics and ecclesiastical art works which adorn many Roman Catholic churches all over South Africa.

With Bishop Mngoma — Zulu born — at its head, Mariannhill remains a dynamic institution that continues to labour quietly in the service of the community, upholding and extending the traditions it has established. Now more than a century and a decade old, the mission has branches spread widely over Natal, all dedicated to the service of the country and its people.

(Above left)
A chapel built after World War I in gratitude for the salvation of Mariannhill from anti-German mobs which attempted to march on the mission staffed largely by Germans

(Above)
A small sculpture set into the wall above the entrance to the monastery

All Saints Church
Ladysmith

(Right) Lych gate entrance to the church; a memorial to men of the district who fell in the First World War

(Above)
All Saints Church on the main street through Ladysmith

Without the famous Siege at the turn of the century, Ladysmith would probably have remained an obscure and unknown hamlet in the Natal midlands. It was a handful of Boers who, at the turn of the century, rocketed the place to fame by confining several thousand British troops within the town for 120 days, and who, by so doing, ensured Ladysmith a permanent niche in the history of South Africa.

Nothing has happened since to alter the town's association with past battles, and, inevitably, much of that history has rubbed off on to All Saints Church which, though damaged, lived through the Siege and the Anglo-Boer War.

Many places of worship in South Africa are far older than All Saints Church in Ladysmith, but, it may be argued, very few more amply reflect the history of their environment than this fine stone-built Anglican Church of the Province of South Africa.

When Colenso, Bishop of Natal, visited the tiny "neat hamlet" of Ladysmith in 1854, he found that in the absence of a venue for worship and minister of their own, the English worshipped in the Dutch Church. The first site granted for the erection of an English church was considered unsuitable and was later exchanged for another where a small church was built, part of which, in 1869, was incorporated into the walls of the town's early defences.

It was not until October 1882, however, that the foundation stone of a new Anglican church was laid, the ceremony being performed by the Governor of Natal, Sir Henry Bulwer.

Ladysmith's position astride natural routes to the interior ensured its development and the early growth soon created a need for a larger place of worship. With money collected in South Africa and Britain in memory of the 3 037 soldiers and many civilians who had died in the Siege, the church of All Saints was extended by the addition of a chancel and a transept, enlarging what is now the nave of the present cruciform building. The enlarged church was consecrated in 1904.

Today All Saints is significant not least for the many war memorials which grace it with solemn dignity. The earliest of these is a memorial to 21 soldiers wounded in the epic battle of Isandlwana against the Zulus and who died in the military hospital at Ladysmith. The inscription is a poignant one. It reads:

> To the Memory of Twenty-one
> British Soldiers
> who died in this town during the
> Zulu War 1879.
> This Tablet is Erected by one
> who nursed them.
> Sister Emma Durham R.R.C.

(Top left) Memorial to those men of the Eighteenth Hussars who died in South Africa during the Boer War

(Top right) The Boer shell which struck the church during the famous Siege, now grouted into the wall of the porch

(Right) Memorial to soldiers wounded in the Zulu War of 1879 who died in the hospital in Ladysmith

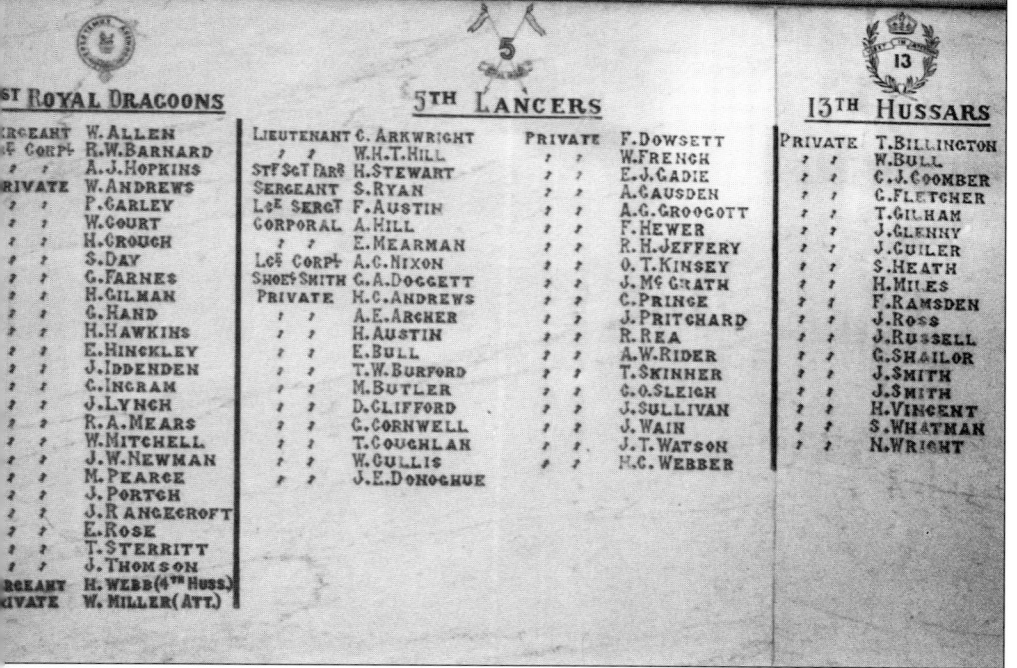

(Below) Some of the British regimental plaques, set in the transepts, memorials to those killed during the Siege of Ladysmith and in the relief of the town

The walls of both transepts are lined with marble plaques inscribed, regiment by regiment, with the names of those who fell during the Siege, each plaque neatly headed by the badge of the regiment.

A tablet close to the magnificently carved pulpit of English oak bears the inscription:

> Father in Thy gracious keeping,
> Leave we now Thy soldiers sleeping.
> Requiescat in Pace.

The fabric of the building bears the scars of its own wounds during the Siege. Of the estimated 15 000 shells which the Boers pumped into a beleaguered Ladysmith during the four months of the summer of 1899-1900, 70 burst near All Saints Church. One actually struck and damaged the porch which, now repaired, has the remains of that shell grouted into the wall in the centre of a plaque telling the story. Close to the porch a small obelisk bears the names of men of Britain's Eighteenth Hussars who died in South Africa during the Anglo-Boer War of 1899-1902.

Among many magnificent stained-glass windows which adorn the church are two depicting "War" and "Peace"; a memorial to men of the Nineteenth Hussars who fell during the Siege and in the relief of the beleaguered garrison.

With Ladysmith the headquarters of the Second Battalion of the Royal Natal Carbineers, the Regiment has inevitably become closely associated with All Saints Church. A brass plaque honours those Carbineers who fell during the Anglo-Boer War. The reredos is a memorial to a prominent citizen of Ladysmith and a church warden of All Saints who served in the regiment during the historic Siege. There is also a memorial to a Carbineer who was killed in the Native Rebellion of 1906.

After the Second World War, the First and Second Battalions of the Regiment were amalgamated and the Colour of the Second Battalion was laid up in All Saints where it is now preserved in a glass case in the north transept.

Battles and military actions in this region of the placid Natal midlands may perhaps have given too strong a military bias to Ladysmith's history. That is debatable. For its part, however, All Saints remains quintessentially a "soldier's church" — perhaps more than any other in South Africa.

Griqua National Independent Church
Kokstad

(Above)
The Griqua National Independent Church building in the centre of Kokstad

As a tribal group, the Griquas came into being largely as a result of miscegenation between passing sailors and early settlers at the Cape, on the one hand, and slave, Hottentot and Bushman women on the other. These half-castes, divided into two clans, were known first as the Bastard Hottentots until, in 1813, the Reverend John Campbell of the London Missionary Society persuaded them to change the name in order to remove the stigma it implied. They did, and called themselves Griquas.

The leader of one of the clans was a freed slave, Adam Kok, whose followers were predominantly Hottentot. The other clan, under Barend Barends, consisted primarily of persons of mixed European and Hottentot ancestry.

Both clans were essentially nomadic, depending for subsistence on hunting and brigandage, and their roamings were extensive. In a raid against the powerful Matabele in 1831, the Barends clan was virtually wiped out.

In 1825 Adam Kok II, with his tribe, settled at Philippolis. On his death there, the leadership passed to his son, Abraham, who was deposed in favour of a younger brother, who, as Adam Kok III, became chieftain of a clan which then possessed considerable land in the area. The conflict between the brothers and their respective supporters became further exacerbated by other claims and personal factors. Political exploitation which, however otherwise expedient for the whites, later led to the Griquas losing their farms and property. It has been said that "the story of how Adam Kok's Griquas lost their land at Philippolis in the aftermath of the Great Trek is a story of British betrayal."

With Philippolis a part of the newly proclaimed Boer Orange Free State Republic and with the Griqua people deprived of rights there and powerless to protest or to fight, Adam Kok had little option but to seek fresh land elsewhere. The British Government pointed out that the Griquas

were at liberty to possess the unoccupied territory called Nomansland which lay between Natal and the Transkei.

After some consideration, they decided in 1860 to accept the offer and under Adam Kok III set out to cross the 600 kilometres to this new home — in an African Promised Land.

The promise emanated from bureaucratic sources, however. Neither heaven nor government rendered assistance. Along the way, no divine miracle protected these hapless trekkers from continuous Basotho harassment and pillage; no heaven-sent phenomenon appeared suddenly to thwart their enemies.

By any standards, the migration was an undertaking of heroic proportions. More than 2 000 men, women and children set out from Philippolis in over 300 wagons and with some 20 000 head of cattle to cross the south-eastern plains of the Free State. Too poor to afford the grazing and watering charges facing them if they skirted the Drakensberg, they chose to avail themselves of Moshesh's undertaking of safe conduct and to face the rigours of the awesome, dangerous mountain route.

Two years later, with herds greatly depleted, equipment severely reduced and after incredible hardship, the weary survivors descended into the unoccupied land they had been granted and established a settlement on and around Mount Currie, taking ground where they wished. The territory became known as East Griqualand.

Searching for an ordained minister, Adam Kok persuaded the Reverend William Dower of the London Missionary Society to join the community. One of Dower's terms for acceptance was that a proper township be laid out. As a result, land near Mount Currie was surveyed and in 1870 the new township was named Kokstad.

A year after his arrival, in 1871, Dower set about the building of a church. " ... we laid the foundations of the Griqua Church. ... As yet we had received no part of the Church Building Fund, " he wrote, and went on, "... the minister and deacons volunteered to quarry and lay down one hundred loads of building-stone on the site..." Timber for the building was cut locally and brought to the site. Others made bricks. Dower tells: "... Thus a good deal of work was done by voluntary labour, until the 1 340 pounds came to hand, and from that time all work had to be paid for..."

Dower "... personally superintended the whole work, " which, he wrote, "... was done by Griqua workmen until we came to the tower. For work done on it they demanded unreasonable wages, and ever increasing as the danger increased with the height ..."

Eventually the work was completed and the church — still in use — opened in May 1877, which was described as "... a great event in the history of the town."

In September 1880, facing the threat of a Basotho uprising, the church was fortified: windows were barricaded, ditches were dug all around, walls of sandbags were constructed, stores were laid in and preparations were made to accommodate the community in the event of a siege.

Through the decades the Griqua Church has been a silent witness to Kokstad's development. Many generations have prayed there. Significant for its history rather than for its architecture, it has seen the decline of the Griquas as a tribal entity: a people who came into being through a mixture of races, and who, now through a similar process, are diminishing, absorbed into more dominant tribes, their genes scattered but their traits overwhelmed beyond recognition.

The pages of history are filled with similar examples. Studies of natural history tell of species which evolve, live and then are extinct.

This whitewashed Griqua church in the centre of Kokstad, with its square, castellated Norman-style tower and its quaint free-standing wooden belfry and charmingly simple interior, is in danger of being similarly absorbed by the community around it. It is more than just a place of worship. It is a memorial to a vanishing people who were victims of some of the sorrier aspects of the nation's development and who, briefly, have featured in the saga of South Africa's history.

Buddhist Retreat Centre
Ixopo

*(Right)
The stupa on a hillside overlooking the Ulufafa valley*

Standing near the large concrete statue of Buddha on the grassy lawns of the Buddhist Retreat Centre, it is difficult to escape the impression that this was not the precise spot described by Alan Paton in the opening paragraphs of his novel, *Cry, the Beloved Country*. This quiet place is situated in the hills of Natal, and is indeed reached by "a lovely road that runs from Ixopo into the hills..." The whole world around this Centre seems to match Alan Paton's descriptions in that beautiful narrative — except from these lawns it is not "the valley of the Umzimkulu" which is below one, but a deep valley which carries the Ulufafa River to the distant Indian Ocean.

No matter: that is a minor detail. Here too also the "... hills are grass-covered and rolling, and they are lovely beyond any singing of it..." And at this place "... you may hear the forlorn cry of the titihoya, one of the birds of the veld ... and beyond and behind the river, great hill after great hill..." The Centre too looks upon hills which reach with similar majesty into the upland distance.

Writing in 1948, Alan Paton described the texture of those midland hillsides and pleaded that the earth be treated with care and respect. "... The grass is rich and matted, you cannot see the soil..." he wrote, "... Stand unshod upon it, for the ground is holy, being even as it came from the Creator..."

Perhaps it is coincidence: these devout Buddhists in the 1970s set up their Centre of Retreat in those lovely hills, and men and women do indeed now stand unshod upon that precious earth.

Buddhism is not one of the major religions of South Africa. Introduced initially by Chinese immigrants in the early years of the twentieth century, Buddhism — practised mainly by Asians — waned in subsequent decades.

In recent years whites in South Africa have shown increasing interest in Buddhism, however, and, in parallel with communities in other parts of the western world, the numbers of Buddhists in South Africa have increased considerably.

In the past decade several thousands of people have visited the Retreat Centre in Natal which, set in 300 acres of hilly ground, is the largest of three such established centres in the country. Retreats and periods of meditation are held regularly and are well attended. The Centre was founded by a civil engineer in Durban, Louis van Loon, who also established the Buddhist Institute of South Africa.

Buddhism has a long history. In the sixth century BC it evolved from the philosophies of Siddartha Gautama, a wealthy prince who gave up his affluent lifestyle in order to attain spiritual emancipation. He spent many years studying philosophy, practising meditation and yogic disciplines under the most renowned teachers of the day, but finally he concluded that true and utter Enlightenment needed a fresh and radically different approach from traditional religious practices. From then on he became known as Buddha — "the One who is awake", or "the Enlightened One".

A descendant of the Bodhi tree (a species of *Ficus*) under which this enlightenment took place

*(Above)
This statue of Buddha, which stands 5 metres in height, is said to be the largest in the Western world*

(Left)
Rays of the early morning sun brighten the stupa

still grows in Bodh Goya in northern India and a tree of the same species has been planted beside the Buddhist statue at the Retreat Centre in Natal.

The Buddha's philosophy appealed greatly to the masses and quickly became popular in India. King Asoka's adoption of the religion in the third century BC gave it additional prestige. From India the religion spread widely to Burma, Ceylon and Thailand, notwithstanding a revival of Hinduism and the onslaught of savage militant forces which invaded India and which were later followed by Islamic invasions and religious persecution. In spite of these hostile forces, Buddhism spread — further eastwards to China, Tibet, Mongolia, Korea and Japan.

Through the centuries Buddhism has acquired a growing number of adherents in the Western world, especially in the United States. Its tenets of rational enquiry, introspection, self-discipline and pacifism exercise considerable appeal in today's turbulent world.

At the Centre accommodation is available for a limited number of devotees; there are lecture and meditation halls staffed by teachers.

Prominent on the lawns between the buildings, looking out across the magnificent panorama of hills and valleys, is a large concrete statue of a Buddha, 5 metres in height, the largest in the Western world. It was sculpted by Louis van Loon. This is no replica of the popular fat-bellied Buddha which, in fact, is not a representation of the historical Buddha, but rather an image of a jolly and eccentric monk who lived in China in the twelfth century and who has become a popular folk image of good fortune.

This statue is in a more classic mould: a handsome and beautifully proportioned man. Traditionally there are distinguishing features — 32 in all — in any statue of the historical Buddha. Some of these include certain markings on the palms of the hands and soles of the feet, together with long ear lobes and symbolic features on the top of the head.

There are no rigid rules of style in representations of Buddha. It is left to the artistic ingenuity of the individual sculptor to decide how to incorporate the traditional characteristics into his work.

Classically Buddha may be depicted in any of four postures: sitting, standing, walking or lying down. In the sitting posture there are five accepted positions (or *mudras*) for the hands. The statue at the Retreat Centre shows Buddha in the *mudra* of meditation — his hands folded on his lap, sitting in the usual *lotus* position. Traditionally, too, meditation is indicated by the eyes, which are in a half-closed position.

In this statue in Natal, the head-knot is removable. Beneath it is a small cavity containing relics donated by a monastery in Thailand, which are reputed to be part of the remains after Buddha's cremation. They are not ashes — as might be expected — but crystals, which remained as a result of the particular method of cremation.

Interestingly, Buddhists do not worship the Buddha. This statue should therefore be regarded as a symbolic expression not of a person, but of Enlightenment.

High at the end of a tree-covered spur of the hill which juts out over the river valley, the whiteness of a Buddhist *stupa* (or pagoda) stands out against the sky and the rolling, grass-covered hills. Traditionally, the *stupa* — which is the Sanskrit word for a mound — had its origins in ancient Indian communal society about 2 000 years BC, when it marked an area of a village kept sacred for religious ceremonies and rituals.

Buddhists have adapted the traditional earthen mound and through the years have moulded it to a more solid form, adding a number of symbolic features. The *stupa* is often the repository for sacred relics. Today, in the Buddhist countries of the East, there are tens of thousands of *stupas*, the styles and names varying from society to society.

The *stupa* at this Retreat contains no relics. Nor is it an object of worship. This *stupa* is a symbolic structure to emphasise the Buddhist way of life, the tranquillity of its noble setting on the hills emphasising the peace inherent in the religious philosophy it represents.

The Yellowwood Chapel of the Holy Trinity
Bulwer

*(Left)
The Yellowwood Chapel
of the Holy Trinity
at Bulwer*

Bulwer is perched on the lower south slopes of the impressive Amahaqwa Mountain in the verdant midlands of Natal, between Pietermaritzburg and the farming town and holiday resort of Underberg nearer the Drakensberg. It is a friendly little village with a subtle maturity that becomes manifest in its unhurried pace of life, attractive for those with time to spare.

Beside the main road, just beyond the police camp on the southern edge of the village, a sign to the "Holy Trinity Yellowood Church" directs one down a sandy lane which, one soon learns, many years ago was the coaching highway from the capital. The road takes one, beneath a canopy of trees, to the little church standing in a large clearing bordered by tangles of wattle trees and a few tall eucalyptus which mark the limits of the churchyard. Inscriptions on several of the scattered gravestones make it plain that the cemetery is an old one, and the age of the church itself is confirmed by a neatly hand-written notice close to its entrance. It reads:

The little church stands on a site fronting on Waggon Road which was originally the main road from Pietermaritzburg to Himeville in the post-cart era. According to records, the Chapel of the Holy Trinity was built as a church on 24 acres of ground bought and donated to the

community by Mr Pascoe Fenwick of England in 1884. He was a brother-in-law of the Rev Benjamin Markham of Ashton Vale from which farm the yellowwood was cut. The timber for the walls was hand-sawn by William Colville who erected the building. Even the doors are hand-made and the Lych gate is particularly attractive. This yellowwood church is probably the last of its vintage still in regular use. Although isolated, it is never locked and visitors are welcome to enter at will.

In 1989, almost a century after its erection, the church was renovated and re-dedicated, the yellowwood walls being scraped, cleaned and reconditioned so that the natural colours of the heavy old timber baulks of which the church is built gleamed again in splendour.

A plaque at the door records that the Chapel was restored in 1989-1990 by Mr D. Davey of Himeville, the project being financed by Mondi Paper Company Limited, and that the Right Reverend Michael Nuttall, Bishop of Natal, officiated at the dedication ceremony on 8 July 1990.

The straightforward simplicity of the structure makes "architecture" perhaps too grand a word to use in relation to its construction — though its innate "aesthetic appeal" would certainly meet the definition set by Nikolaus Pevsner, an authority on architecture, who, distinguishing "architecture" from "building", wrote that "the term architecture applies only to buildings designed with a view to aesthetic appeal".

(Far left above)
Dates on the gravestones tell the age of this little church

(Left)
The Lych gate opens from the old wagon road

(Far left below)
The yellowwood timber patterns the walls

The chapel is merely two rectangular sections, one smaller than the other, joined together and topped by a sloping corrugated iron roof, common enough in South Africa.

But, notwithstanding the simplicity of its construction, this church has considerable interest — not least for the manner in which the substantial yellowwood baulks have been sawn and then put together to form the walls. The chapel's charm lies not least in the texture, the grain and the colour of the wood and in the skill with which the beams have been arranged to emphasise the beauty of the timber itself. Through the years weathering has bequeathed it a patina of its own.

While the claim of this yellowwood chapel to being "the last of its vintage in regular use" is probably beyond dispute, it is not the only timber church in existence in South Africa. There is another at Redbourne, near Plettenberg Bay (q.v.), which is older than this little place of worship at Bulwer, but which, though often used, is not in regular use.

The quiet appeal and unusual charm of this wooden Chapel of the Holy Trinity are not dependent upon any claim to uniqueness, however. Set in a place of great natural beauty and resting in solitude, it remains not only architecturally interesting but also a living link with the country's pioneering past.

The Soofi Mosque
Ladysmith

(Above)
The Soofi Mosque across the Klip River

The interest and attractiveness of ecclesiastical architecture in South Africa are heightened considerably by the art and styles of the non-Christian religions which have become such a colourful part of the country's cultural heritage.

The general monochrome plainness of design which continues to influence the decoration and appearance of so many Protestant churches in South Africa stems largely from those Calvinistic philosophies of northern Europe which the early settlers brought with them to the Cape and which contrast strongly with the *élan* manifest in places of worship serving Asian South Africans.

This is seen particularly — though not only — in Natal where Indians — both Moslem and Hindu — mainly settled and, to a lesser extent, in the Cape with its communities of peoples whose forefathers came from Malaya.

One of the most interesting and attractive Moslem places of worship in South Africa is undoubtedly the Soofi Mosque in Ladysmith in Natal. Set serenely in an uncluttered space on the south side of the Klip River, away from the centre of the town, it stands out boldly, framed by trees, its ornamental white towers, domes and graceful minarets proud against the low hills behind it. It is the second-largest mosque in South Africa.

While the site has been the centre of Moslem worship in Ladysmith since almost the beginning of this century, the present building there is relatively new.

With considerable wisdom and great foresight, the Moslem community in 1906 selected and developed four acres of ground in an isolated area away from the town where possession was unlikely to be contested, and there, on the high bank of the Klip River, they built a small House of Prayer. In this endeavour the community was guided by Soofi Saheb, who is associated with the construction of a number of mosques in Natal and the Transvaal. When he left Ladysmith, the custody of the mosque passed to another individual and, only later, to the local Moslem community.

In 1959 an Order of the Natal Supreme Court

(Left)
The ornamental gateway to the mosque and the Moslem school

awarded legal title of the ground to the Ladysmith Moslem Trust.

In due course a larger place of worship became necessary. Rather than renovate the existing old building, it was decided to build an entirely new mosque on the site. One of the Trustees, S.M. Seedat, agreed to finance the project, which also included the construction of a Madressa (Moslem school) in the same grounds. The new mosque, completed in 1969, is one of the finest and most attractive in all South Africa. At the same time the Moslem community financed the construction of a sturdy bridge across the river at this spot — a bridge which still serves the entire suburb, now considerably enlarged, and all the people of Ladysmith.

The building of the mosque was supervised by "Chacha" Jumallidin, who brought traditional religious architectural designs from his native India. He had worked on the coal mines in northern Natal before becoming a builder specialising in designing and constructing mosques. With pride Moslems in Ladysmith tell how their mosque was built without the formality of a drawn plan. Jumallidin, who had no formal training either in architecture or building, is said to have sketched lines in the sand for the builders to work on and he supervised each stage of the great task, improvising as the structure developed.

Between the gravelled paths of the present ornamental gardens are grassy patches, rose beds and shrubs and, in traditional style, large ponds painted cool blue, with elegantly decorated fountains.

The interior of the mosque is spacious and airy. Beyond the entrance hall, with its rows of stools and taps where feet are washed before prayers, is the main area of worship. Its floor is rich with colourful, matching prayer mats which, placed close together, give the impression of a single, large and sumptuous carpet of red and gold.

Around the walls, just below the ceiling, is a frieze of circular plaques — 99 in all — with Koranic inscriptions in Arabic dedicated to Allah. Some of the windows are similarly inscribed. The prevailing atmosphere of tranquillity and quiet is conducive to prayer and meditation, the plainness of the interior in contrast with the impressive ornamentation of the many-domed exterior which compels attention — and admiration — from both far and near.

A Drakensberg Country Church
Cathkin Peak

The charm of this small country church lies not least in the manner in which the magnificence of the mountains around it has been brought into the interior area of worship. Here there is no need for man-made decorated windows, for gilded baroque statues of clay or stone. Painted replicas and illustrations of nature's beauty are made superfluous by the splendour of the surrounding scenery and its reflected presence in the church itself.

It is the embodiment of the psalmist's credo: "I will lift up mine eyes to the hills from whence cometh my help..."

A simple A-frame structure with a steep, thatched roof, this church, seating only about 30 people, is available to Christian worshippers of all denominations. Set in the foothills of the Drakensberg, it has a large window of plain glass above the altar, quartered by stays in the form of a cross, which frames a magnificent view of the towering Champagne Castle, one of the noblest and most spectacular peaks of the whole mountain range.

Its construction in 1970 was the inspiration of Roland Smith and his wife, owners then of the country hotel, El Mirador, in the grounds of which the church stands. He designed and built it himself to serve visitors to the several holiday farms and hotels in the area and to provide a place for quiet meditation with God "even amidst the hustle and bustle of a holiday."

For many years Roland Smith preached there on Sunday mornings and so popular were those services that loud-speakers often were needed outside the little chapel for the overflow of worshippers who sat on the lawns under the trees. The church soon became well known and the adjacent hotel was often used for church

(Above)
This charming little A-frame country church is set against the background of the majestic Drakensberg

conferences, many of which were attended by Christian leaders from overseas as well as from many parts of South Africa. The chapel is a popular venue for weddings.

Though itself not old, the chapel has several links with early history. The pews come from the gallery of the original old Methodist church which was built in 1820 in West Street in Durban. They were transported to El Mirador on lorries with the help of farmers in the area.

The font was given by the father of a child baptised there. The lectern was donated by a visitor who fell down a mountainside while climbing in the Drakensberg and who, "having bounced off three rock-levels", survived without serious injury. The lectern is a symbol of his gratitude to the God who spared his life.

The simplicity of the church's construction is appropriate to the calm of its rural setting amid flower beds, green lawns and shady trees, a place of great beauty and deep serenity; looking out across a wide valley to the towering mountains. It is a moving experience to sit in silence in the tiny chapel at any time of the day and the night and to reflect upon the infinite majesty of those great peaks which, when neither wild storms nor swirling mist conceal the heights, peer down through sunlight and darkness into this holy place. Through that large plain window, on a clear night, how rich it is to watch the stars in their courses and, too, in the freshness of the morning, to see the first sunbeams of the new day strike — silent and pink — on the dark rocks high above the quiet shadows of the still-sleeping valleys below.

"... I will lift up mine eyes to the hills ... "

(Above left)
The church bell shelters under the eaves of the thatched roof

(Left)
The splendour of the ceaseless parade of hours and seasons with the constantly changing colours and shadows on the mountains far surpasses the beauty of any man-made adornment

The Shree Poongavana Amman Temple
Durban

(Left) Bright sculptural adornments edge the roof of the temple

Unlike many of the baroque churches of Europe, Christian places of worship in South Africa generally have little — if any — sculptural ornamentation. There are no bizarre gargoyles on their façades and columns to ward off the Devil, as in some of the great medieval cathedrals of Britain and Europe. There are no knights and heroes in stone and bronze sleeping silently and eternally on hallowed tombs, or memorial statues to remind congregations and visitors of the feats of famous rulers, brave soldiers, intrepid explorers, poets and other noble and famous men whose various achievements have contributed to the nation's progress and the history of Christianity.

Is it that we shave no such heroes? Is it that, in this sense, our perceptions of human greatness have not matured — or that they lie in other directions, awaiting perspective to crystallise them?

In South Africa it is mainly in the Roman Catholic churches that we find tangible representations of Christ and the Holy Family — mainly in the form of the Crucifixion. Elsewhere few paintings and carvings help make manifest the Creation and the wonder of the beliefs which Christians have accepted and practised through almost 20 centuries.

But if South Africa's Christian churches are deficient in ornamentation of this sort, the Indian temples of Natal certainly make amends for that lack. Most temples are richly endowed with traditional oriental art, much of it bizarre to Western eyes. And while the plain white of the temple figures of the Tamils modestly invites attention to their sculpture and form rather than to

*(Right)
The temple viewed from
the firewalling terrace
in the foreground*

colour, the strong and gaudy hues of Hindu sculptures tend to assault the viewer with a ferment of juxtaposed colours, lively, strong and vibrant.

The Shree Poongavana Amman temple in Bellair Road, Durban, is such a place of worship. Recently renovated, the freshness of the paintwork currently gives the colours yet further force.

Just when the first communal Hindu temple was built in Natal remains a matter of some debate: probably about the middle of the 1870s. This temple was certainly one of the early Hindu places of worship in South Africa, built by an Indian named Poonsamy for the owner of a property, an ex-indentured Indian, Moongalam. Sited on a terrace gouged out of a hillside, this temple embodies many features of Hindu architecture.

From the front an unusual barrel-vaulted roof leads back to domes of beautiful proportions, their bases and sides richly decorated with a profusion of figures of gods, birds and animals. The frieze continues — interrupted here and there — to the pediment above a shallow verandah at the front, itself alive with more figures and animals, closely packed, all guarded by bizarre, heavy-toothed lions peering from above them.

It is a lively scene of frozen animation, gods and mythical animals in profusion, gaudy peacocks, sacred white cattle, monkeys and mermaids.

The shrine is Kali's, one of the female gods in the Hindi pantheon, whose effigy rests in the innermost sanctum of this temple. In this form she is hideous and terrifying: black-skinned and bloodthirsty with four arms. She also has a more benign aspect, however. For women especially she is the supreme and divine mother, and it is from Kali that Hindu women seek by prayer the gift of children.

Below the temple on a flat grassy terrace, about the size of a football field, the annual fire-walking ceremony takes place. The motives for participating in this ritual vary from person to person. The act is often undertaken as a form of religious purification, or as a plea for good crops and good fortune.

Fire-walking is an ancient custom, and one not limited to India. It was practised also by numbers of other peoples, including the ancient Greeks and Chinese. Its form varies, but in the main consists of walking barefooted across burning embers or red-hot stones. The devout and those who have faith are said not to suffer from the fires and, while burns do occur, for reasons not medically understood injuries are infrequent.

The Church of the Good Shepherd
Hlabisa

(Below) Carved panels on a door of the church show events in the life of Christ and His Crucifixion

There cannot be many churches in the world built especially to provide scope for the work of an artist: generally the artist is called in to supply whatever decoration and ornamentation may be required once the building is completed. It must be rare for an artist to be able to claim that a place of worship had been built expressly to provide him with an opportunity of exercising his talents.

But the Roman Catholic Mission Church of the Good Shepherd at Hlabisa in KwaZulu is such a place. A Zulu sculptor, Bernard Gcwenza, born in that area, was the artist for whom the church was expressly built. His wood carvings are a feature of an otherwise large and rather plain building, part of a complex set on a hillside looking down on the untidy little village of Hlabisa, nothing more than a handful of odd buildings straggling along both sides of a dusty country road a kilometre or so below.

The church was constructed by members of the congregation from concrete blocks made on the spot and faced with a scrubbed terasso finish of fluoride pebbles which are found in the vicinity and which, with their wide range of delicate colours, give life to the surface of the dull blocks.

There is a broad, roofed verandah all round the building and the church grounds are enclosed by a low stone wall. The section of the enclosure behind the building consists of a semi-circular roofed colonnade with an altar at its centre, looking over a grassy space, a covered arena for open-air services. Its facing wall is decorated with religious scenes carved in stone, set into the grey cement wall and linked by a series of black line-drawings illustrating the Seven Sorrows of Mary, mother of Christ — the religious series known as the *Via Matris*. These carvings and subdued, understated drawings are the work of another local African artist, Ruben Xulu.

A tall circular bell-tower at the front, surmounted by a Cross, is built of roughly dressed local stone, its texture contrasting with the smooth cement blocks of the main building from which it is separated.

The prevailing peace and tranquillity of the enclosure is emphasised by the presence of two or three free-ranging cows whose grazing keeps the veld grass there from becoming too unruly.

The mission at Hlabisa had been established for several decades by the time the church came to be built between 1961 and 1963. For a number of years it was served by the German Benedictines

(Facing page) Panels on the inside of a door, carved by Gcwenza, illustrate biblical subjects as well as activities at the Hlabisa mission

(Left) The Crucifixion of Christ; detail of a panel carved by Bernard Gcwenza

until it was taken over in 1951 by the Servite Order from America under the leadership of Father Edwin Kinch. It was his inspired understanding and personal encouragement which led to the flowering of the work of Bernard Gcwensa and another, younger artist, Ruben Xulu, who lived near the mission and who learned much of his craftsmanship from his elder — and self-taught — colleague. It was Father Kinch also who provided Gcwensa with the wood and the tools for his carvings and who explained the religious significance of whatever subjects he suggested might be tackled.

Neither Gcwensa nor Xulu was literate in the conventional sense. Gcwensa had passed only two lower grades at school and could not speak English. Xulu had been both deaf and dumb since the age of ten, when he was purported to have been overtaken by some strange, mysterious and unexplained phenomenon in a forest.

Both artists died young. Ruben Xulu was mysteriously murdered.

Impressed by Gcwensa's art, Father Kinch took a specimen to Professor Jack Grossert, then head of Bantu Art Education in Natal, who at the time happened to be collecting art works for an exhibition. At once Grossert included the piece in the exhibition, where it won a prize. But, more than that, it demonstrated Gcwensa's artistic ability beyond the limits of Hlabisa.

A suggestion that the Zulu artist be sent overseas for training was at once stamped on by Professor Grossert. Not only would Gcwensa's lack of English handicap — and discourage — him, but Grossert believed the imposition of an alien culture would stifle his incentive and natural talent. He suggested that to encourage the artist further it would be more appropriate to provide greater opportunity for the development of his native art and latent talent — such as building a church for him to decorate in his own natural environment.

Clearly the wisdom of that decision has been made manifest in the magnificence of Gcwensa's carvings in the Church of the Good Shepherd at Hlabisa and, too, in the art there of his deaf-mute friend and compatriot, Ruben Xulu.

The interior of the mission church is dominated by a large crucifix carved by Gcwensa above the altar. The doors consist of panels in which more of his fine carvings illustrate not only biblical subjects but also a number of the mission's activities.

The doors of the confessionals are also beautifully decorated — with carvings of saints — while there is a fine wooden statue of the Madonna as well as representations of the Stations of the Cross, a traditional subject rather unusually depicted here by carved figures, unframed, simply attached to the walls of the church.

The plain simplicity of this mission church is relieved by the fine ornamentation which these impressive carvings provide. With a unique African flavour, they are refreshingly different in style and treatment from the often overdone popular traditional European church art.

The Sri-Sri Radha-Radhanath Temple of Understanding
Durban

(Above)
The gleaming towers of the Hare Krishna temple

Though Hare Krishna beliefs reach back many thousands of years, the life of the formalised Hare Krishna movement is still counted in decades plus a few odd years rather than in the millennia or centuries by which the ages of the more historically established religions and sects are measured. But the growth in the numbers of Hare Krishna adherents since its inception in 1966 has been phenomenal.

Its roots reach into ancient Hindu customs and traditions, while the dress of its members is similar to that worn by Hindus. They also observe the four traditional Hindu stages of life, as well as accepting a modified caste system — based, however, on personal aptitude rather than on social levels at birth. As with the Hindus, meat and alchohol are forbidden.

Formally known as the International Society for Krishna Consciousness (ISKCON), the Hare Krishna movement was founded in 1966 in the United States by A.C. Bhaktivedanta, an Indian who had emigrated to America and who, in the movement he founded, became known as Swami Prabhupada. It was he who, during a visit to South Africa in 1975, decided that a branch should be established here, and this opulent, extravagant edifice at Chatsworth in Natal — the Sri-Sri Radha-Radhanath Temple of Understanding — is the result. It has been described as "a unique architectural masterpiece heralding a modern renaissance of ancient Vedic culture and philosophy."

The building was designed by a young Austrian architect who, having studied in India, became a

*(Left)
A remarkably
lifelike effigy of
Swami Prabhupada,
founder of ISKCON*

Krishna devotee and, after his religious initiation in 1977, adopted the name Rajaram Das. The temple in Natal was built by local devotees who did all but the more technically difficult work, which was contracted out to specialists. The result is said to bond architectural features from the orient with those of the west and to link the past with the present and, with them, to influence the future. Construction took more than four years and the final cost is said to have amounted to some several million rands.

It is a large and unusual building of several storeys, white and gold and with panels of shiny stainless steel that flash in the sunlight. Colourful gardens surround the temple and paved walks and bridges cross the broad encircling moat. A ring of large glass windows below roof level eliminates any look of heaviness in the structure while three decorated hexagonal towers reach up from the roof, drawing the eye to the heavens.

Several floors are set aside to accommodate resident devotees and also to provide for tourists.

The main focus is upon the temple chamber, however; a spacious octagonal hall well lit by large windows on all sides. At one end the altar is set against richly ornamented panels. Coloured marble and mirrors are used to great decorative effect. The panelled ceiling is made colourful by large religious pictures, painted by local artists in an oriental idiom.

Set into an alcove near the main entrance to the chamber is an extremely lifelike effigy of Swami Prabhupada. On his forehead he carries the painted stripes that are the traditional Vishnu

symbol. Sitting in calm contemplation on a red-cushioned throne, the figure watches quietly over the temple chamber where devotees come to pray.

Chanting is believed to purify the soul — and this is ritually practised daily by members, both in groups as well as individually.

Krishna is a divine and much revered figure, a reincarnation of the Hindu god, Vishnu. The central figure in a number of religious cults, he has inspired the writing of much religious poetry, while music and legends about his spirited youthful years feature prominently in oriental art and culture. Some of these legends are depicted in the decorative painted panels on the ceiling in the central prayer chamber of this modern temple.

Krishna the god is often portrayed as a shepherd in rustic surroundings, admired by adoring shepherdesses. This is generally interpreted as being symbolic of the continuing love between God and mankind, the link between heaven and earth, between the spirit and the flesh.

The architecture of this modern temple reflects much of the religion's traditional ancient symbolism. Geometric patterns are used to signify human qualities — and weaknesses: circles are deemed to represent ignorance, for example; a triangle expresses passion and action; a square represents goodness and knowledge. The octagon is Krishna's own symbol — seen in the configuration of the central temple chamber itself.

The waters of the encircling moat here symbolise the unceasing movement of life, death and reincarnation. To enter the temple one crosses a bridge over that water, symbolising that in entering the sanctuary one crosses from this world into the spiritual calm of another.

(Above left)
View of the front of the main assembly hall. The picture above it was painted locally

(Above)
Krishna portrayed in rustic surroundings with an adoring shepherdess

The Llandaff Oratory
Van Reenen

(Left)
The altar and sanctuary of this small Roman Catholic oratory

On the main highway from southern Africa's hinterland to the continent's south-eastern seaboard, the little country town of Van Reenen straddles the border between the provinces of the Orange Free State and Natal. It is here that the flat lands of the highveld suddenly begin to fall away down the steep escarpment to the green hills and the undulating countryside which reaches eastwards to the Indian Ocean.

Now cramped by encroaching commercial buildings and tucked away from sight behind a busy filling station on the western side of the highway, is the little red brick Roman Catholic chapel which claims to be "the smallest church in the world" and the only Roman Catholic church in the world which is privately owned.

Endless numbers of travellers and curious passers-by turn from the highway each day to see this diminutive place of worship, which has become well known throughout the land. Some 75 000 people are said to visit it each year.

It is not any particular architectural feature that attracts so many visitors, nor is it any important historical association: the chapel was built by a father as a memorial to a son who lost his life tragically in an accident down a coal mine. In that sense, the chapel has a powerful and wide appeal, but there is little doubt that to sightseers the appeal now lies almost solely in its claim to being the smallest church in the world.

Inside, on the right-hand side of the entrance to the church, a framed typewritten page surmounted by a small photograph of the church gives the background to its origins. The tale is endearingly related in the first person by the chapel itself.

It records how Maynard Mathew, a Roman Catholic, having lost his son, wished to place a plaque in a Catholic church in memory of the young

(Left)
The front view and entrance of this tiny memorial place of worship

man, Llandaff, but this wish was denied him. Aggrieved, he built this little church himself and there placed the memorial plaque.

Small though it is, the chapel "... which seats just eight has all the vestments of its bigger brothers...."

Gilded letters, incised into the black marble of a plaque, spell out the father's love for the son he lost. It reads:

> To the Glory of God
> and
> In Loving Memory of
> LLANDAFF MATHEW
> Who gave his life to save those of
> others at Burnside Colliery on
> March 19th 1925.
> Aged 28.
>
> R. I. P.

The official report of the Government Mining Inspector investigating this fatal accident reveals that Llandaff was crushed in a fall of rock after a blasting operation, had his pelvis broken and died in hospital the following day.

The brick tower above the chapel's entrance is surmounted by a Celtic Cross, while at the apex of the gable at the other end of the green-tiled roof there is a smaller, plain Cross.

Two windows, not large, on each side wall provide light; two roundels, one to the left and the other to the right above the altar and set in the small angular three-sided sanctuary, light the far end of the interior. The side windows are leaded. The plainness of their white mottled glass is relieved by a simple floral design in the centre of each and both windows are rimmed in crimson.

The *Guinness Book of Records* would seem now to contest the Oratory's claim to being the smallest church in the world. In Malaga in Spain there is an old Catholic chapel — a monument to Christopher Columbus — which is said to have a floor area of only 1,96 square metres, which is about one-fifth the size of this place of worship in South Africa.

No matter: the little private oratory at Van Reenen retains a charm of its own — whether or not it is indeed the smallest church in the world. Above all, it is — and will forever remain — a moving memorial to a father's love for a lost son.

The Subrahmanya Temple
Tinley Manor

(Below)
The decorated tower of this Hindu place of worship, with colourful figures created by Yellappa Govender

This colourful Hindu temple, set on a levelled grassy patch in a rural setting close to the main road between Ballito and Stanger, has been described as "Architecturally and sculpturally one of the most remarkable temples on the Natal coast."

Not by any means as large or as opulent as many others in the region, the temple at Tinley Manor makes its statement through the brilliance and the quaintness of the colourful ornamentation which decks its exterior. More than 150 figures of Hindu deities, humans and animals, inoffensively and naively eccentric in form, adorn the tower, the roof and the front of this modest temple building: tigers with swishing tails, heavily maned lions with fiercely prominent teeth, grotesque elephants and twin-headed bulls, men in bright military uniforms, men devoutly at prayer, and many more.

The building of this Shiva temple commenced in 1913 and was completed in the following year. It was carried out wholly by the community under the supervision of three Indians who, without formal training in the field of building, had developed the necessary skills.

The idea of building a temple for the area is said to have come from Perumal Naiker and it was he who was largely responsible for collecting the money for its construction. Others, with the necessary knowledge, designed the building and supervised progress. Bricks were made by members of the community, working mostly at the weekends. Another self-taught artisan, Yellappa Govender, was responsible for the sculpture and himself created many of the decorative figures while supervising the making of others.

The temple itself consists of an open forecourt, seasonally roofed against the summer's heat by palm leaves arranged on a framework of poles. It is overlooked by the customary *kodi*, a flagpole. From the forecourt one enters a large room which in turn leads into a smaller room reserved for men and priests alone, and, finally, to the *cella* where the images of the particular deities are kept.

Above the *cella*, at the end of the low, tin-roofed building, is the tower with its horizontal rows of ornate, colourful concrete sculptures, one above the other in Dravidian style.

The story is told that in 1929 a high priest, brought especially to halt the spread of malaria then ravaging the community, noticed a flaw in the ritual portrayal of Subrahmanya, the temple's chief deity, and instructed that the idol be removed. Though this was done, malaria continued nevertheless to take its unhappy toll of the community.

More recently when three young devotees of the community were tragically drowned at Tinley

*(Far right above and below)
Details of some of the
figures which adorn
the temple*

*(Right)
The Subrahmanya temple*

*(Right)
A new shrine, created
by a mysterious fire*

Manor Beach, a tall eucalyptus tree beside the temple mysteriously caught fire at the top and for 14 days burned slowly and steadily downwards until, less than a metre from the ground, the fire went out, leaving only a charred stump.

The circumstances of that fire are shrouded in mystery, which has led many to regard the occurrence as supernatural. Many now come to pray at what seems to have become a new shrine. The stump is freshly decorated each day with a red cloth and flowers, and camphor and matches are placed there for the use of visitors.

In the minds of many devotees the fire which began strangely and spontaneously high in the gum tree is linked with the sad drownings of the three young men of that temple community at Tinley Manor.

132 Nederduitsch Hervormde Kerk
Potchefstroom

135 The Great Synagogue
Johannesburg

138 St Andrew's Presbyterian Church
Germiston

141 Nederduitse Gereformeerde Kerk
Pretoria East

144 The Zion Christian Church
Moria

146 The Greek Orthodox Church
Pretoria

148 Nederduitse Gereformeerde Kerk
Lydenburg

151 The Mariaman Hindu Temple
Pretoria

154 Nederduitse Gereformeerde Kerk
Middelburg

157 The Lion *Shul*
Johannesburg

159 The Lutheran Mission
Botshabelo

162 The Zionist Church
Wakkerstroom

164 Universiteitsoord
Pretoria

167 Rhema Church
Randburg

170 An Interdenominational Chapel
Verwoerdburg

(Facing page)

*The Nederduitse Gereformeerde Kerk
at Lydenburg*

Transvaal

Nederduitsch Hervormde Kerk
Potchefstroom

Founded on the banks of the Mooi River by the pioneer leader, Andries Potgieter, from whom Potchefstroom took its name ("The stream where Potgieter is chief"), this town in the western Transvaal claims many historical "firsts". Settled by the Voortrekkers in 1838, it was the first town north of the Vaal River and for a while it was the capital of the fledgling first South African Republic until Pretoria, becoming more centrally situated as settlement extended, assumed that responsibility. It was in Potchefstroom that the first church congregation across the Vaal came into being and the Transvaal's first place of worship was built.

To raise money for its construction, subscription lists were opened in November 1841: four months later a council was set up to co-ordinate the affairs of the fledgling congregation and to build a church. Soon afterwards, in March 1842, the first church gatherings and services in the new territory followed. They were held under canvas stretched between wagons in the centre of the small town. For some years, services continued to be held in this fashion while the building of a permanent place of worship went ahead. Finally completed, it was consecrated by the Reverend John Murray, then minister at Bredasdorp in the Cape. This original building, cruciform in design, was surrounded by a wall with loop-holed embrasures in case of hostile attack.

The building served a multiplicity of purposes. During the week it was used as a school and, for some years, was where the governing body of the first South African Republic periodically met in session. It was in that church, too, in January 1857 that Marthinus Wessels Pretorius was sworn in as the Republic's first State President.

(Above)
The gallery, with the pipes of the old imported organ and wrought-iron balustrade

It was not long, however, before the building became too small for the growing community and, on 26 December 1859, President Pretorius, together with the Reverend Dirk van der Hoff, first minister of the Potchefstroom congregation (1853-1881), laid the foundation stone of a new and larger church — which, with some later structural alterations and additions, still serves the community.

Civil strife interrupted its construction and consecration was delayed until February 1866. A fine carved pulpit of pine and yellowwood, which was brought by ox-wagon from Pietermaritzburg at that time, is still in use — the oldest in the Transvaal.

The settlement expanded and, as a traveller wrote, Potchefstroom had become "a rather nice looking town..." where "...churches are plentiful: English, Dutch and Congregational places of worship."

Like many of the country's older churches and, too, as its predecessor had been, the Hervormde Kerk is cruciform in shape. The walls, now painted cream, are of locally made sun-baked bricks on stone foundations. The original thatched roof has been replaced by corrugated iron, painted black, from which a tall, silvered spire reaches high into the sky, topped by a shiny weathercock. Inside, the beams supporting the roof are of yellowwood, while galleries have been added to both wings and, too, at the back of the church where there is a fine, decorated organ — now electrically operated — with the original wood of its pipes replaced by metal. The heavy instrument was imported from London in about 1890, shipped to the Cape, there off-loaded and sent by train to Vryburg, the nearest

(Above)
Bust of Dominee Dirk van der Hoff, the congregation's first minister: sculpted by Coert Steynberg, 1951

(Left)
The fine carved pulpit, brought by ox-wagon from Pietermaritzburg where it was made

railway station at the time, and from there was taken by ox-wagon to Potchefstroom, where it was assembled by the organist himself — with the help only of the accompanying instruction manuals!

An English visitor to Potchefstroom in 1882 described the town as a "... quaint little place, with its long row of unevenly built houses, its broad, sandy street, over which the weeping willows arched and cast their welcome shade..."

Today the church is set amid pleasant gardens and the lawns of the Church Square in the centre of modern Potchefstroom. Behind it is a new hall, next to which, on a stand of sturdy wooden beams, is a large cast-iron bell given to the church in 1912 by admirers in Holland.

At the east end of the building, in front of the main entrance facing the Town Hall across the street, is a bronze bust of Dominee Dirk van der Hoff, the church's first minister. It was sculpted by Coert Steynberg and erected in Potchefstroom in 1952. On the wall beside the steps a bronze plaque, placed by the National Monuments Council, briefly relates the history of the church's early foundation.

While not especially significant for its architecture, this church is one to be cherished for its considerable historical value.

The Great Synagogue
Johannesburg

(Above)
The Great Synagogue facing Wolmarans Street

The long-established participation of Jewish people in Europe's diamond and jewellery trade had led many to extend their interests to South Africa when diamonds were discovered at Kimberley. By the time of the rich gold discoveries on the Witwatersrand in 1886 — almost 20 years later — the success of many of Kimberley's pioneering entrepreneurs, including a number of Jewish financiers, enabled them to turn their business interests to the new gold fields of the Transvaal. The early availability of investment capital gave the new industry a valuable start that set the Witwatersrand on its golden pathway to success.

Thus it was that in the year following the discovery of gold, there was a large enough Jewish community in the shanty gold-mining town to form a congregation asking for their own place of worship.

Just as they had been closely associated from the start with the history and development of Kimberley and contributed significantly to the success of the diamond industry, so Jewish people were involved in the growth of Johannesburg, there also contributing to the success and prosperity of the Witwatersrand gold industry.

Their presence on the Witwatersrand was quickly recognised by the Government of the Zuid Afrikaansche Republiek in the grant of plots for a burial ground. Historical records show that in July 1887, soon after that gift of ground, 88 Jews met in Wainstein's store on Market Square and formed the Witwatersrand Goldfields Jewish Association which, *inter alia*, assumed responsibility for the upkeep of the burial ground. Two months later, with the advent of the traditional High Festival Services of Rosh Ha'shanah, the Association arranged the celebration of those Services — the first regular Jewish services held on the Witwatersrand.

It is interesting indeed to note — especially in the light of later attitudes — that those first services were held in the Rand Club since there was no other venue large enough to house the 500 worshippers who were expected to attend.

Early in the following year the Jewish Association changed its designation to the Hebrew Congregation and this body went ahead with the building of a synagogue on the two plots which had been allocated to it in President Street. That synagogue served the community for several

*(Right)
This Ark set a new tradition by facing north towards Jerusalem*

decades until the site was sold and the building was demolished in 1926.

A schism in the local Jewish community in 1891 led to the formation of the Johannesburg Hebrew Congregation, whereupon the older body chose to alter its name to the Witwatersrand Old Hebrew Congregation. The two bodies maintained their individuality until 1915 when they joined forces to become the United Hebrew Congregation of Johannesburg. Through the personal association of one of its members, Bension Aaron, with President Kruger — whose election campaign he had managed in Johannesburg — the Johannesburg Hebrew Congregation was granted four plots of ground at the corner of Joubert and De Villiers Streets on which to build its synagogue. Situated near the old Park Street railway station, it became known as the Park Street Synagogue.

It was ceremoniously inaugurated by President Kruger himself, who stood bare-headed in the Synagogue as he delivered his address in Dutch and said, "I open this synagogue in the name of Jesus Christ!"

The *General Directory of Johannesburg* for 1910 remarked that "... places of worship are numerous but no religious buildings of any importance have been erected except the Jewish synagogue".

Urban development led to the building's being sold in 1912, the site later being incorporated into Johannesburg's new railway station. With the demise of the Park Street Synagogue, thought was given to the building of a new place of worship and a site in Wolmarans Street, bounded by Claim, Quartz and Smit Streets, was selected by the architect Herman Kallenbach for the purpose.

The new synagogue, it was decided, should accommodate 850 men and 550 women. Its cost should not exceed 18 000 pounds. A competition for its design brought no less than 22 entries, and the winner received a prize of 50 guineas. The top three architects were asked to amend their plans and from those the final choice was made. The winner was Theophile Schaerer, a Swiss architect, whose scheme was estimated to cost 20 407 pounds.

In the course of his travels Schaerer had been immensely impressed by the architectural

magnificence of the Santa Sophia Mosque in Constantinople. Originally built in the sixth century as a Christian church, its conversion to a Moslem shrine when the Turks captured the city in 1453 did nothing to alter its significance as the finest jewel of Byzantine architecture.

The magnificence of that historic building so impressed Schaerer that he embodied its basic design in his plans for this new synagogue — scaled down proportionally to meet local circumstances — its main feature being a central dome flanked by two smaller domes on the wings.

It is perhaps not without wry interest that this Jewish place of worship in Johannesburg was designed on the lines of a Christian church built in the Middle East 14 centuries earlier and which, some 900 years later, had been converted to a Moslem mosque.

The foundation stone was laid in September 1913 by the legendary Sammy Marks. World War I interrupted the building when the architect returned to Switzerland to join the army and completion was delayed until 1918.

The Wolmarans Street synagogue was the first in Johannesburg to set the Ark facing north — towards Jerusalem — a practice which was later followed by many other synagogues throughout the country.

The building is an impressive one, its appearance reflecting the strength of its character. Occupying the greater part of a large site bounded by four busy streets, the Star of David adorning the apex of its metal sheathed dome, its presence proclaims the strength and faith of the community it serves.

Its interior is large and airy; well lit by large windows around the base of the central dome. The dark, solid woodwork shows the patina of its decades and the plainness of the interior serves to emphasise the richness of the curtain screening the Ark and the splendour of the gold mosaic above the sacred recess.

The large entrance foyer, with its floor of black and white marble, houses a number of commemorative plaques and memorials that crystallise events in the history of the Jewish community on the Witwatersrand and pay tribute to the many personalities who have added to its lustre.

Of the many places of worship which have been established through the decades to serve the growing Jewish community, the Great Synagogue is the doyen of them all, the size of its congregation now multiplied manyfold. Itself creating history, it has also been a witness to the march of history, both within and beyond South Africa.

(Above left)
The Bema

(Above)
A memorial in the entrance foyer

St Andrew's Presbyterian Church
Germiston

(Far right above) The forward section of the church's octagonal interior

(Right) Stained-glass window by Estelle Vallé

(Far right below) The foundation stone, laid in 1905, set into the front of the building

It was the large number of Scottish miners who came to the Witwatersrand when gold was discovered that gave impetus to the early establishment of Presbyterian congregations there. One of these was formed in Germiston, the name of the settlement deriving from the birthplace of one of its Scots founders.

It was the Presbyterian congregation which, in 1890, built the first church in Germiston — and which, furthermore, also built the town's first school. Known at first as the Germiston Presbyterian Church, it later took on the more Scottish name of St Andrew's, and now is generally known by a combination of the two.

With seating for 300 worshippers, that first church was a wood and iron building, not unusual in those pioneering days, erected on one of four plots donated to the congregation. Growth of the town made the site a valuable one and, to ease the financial strains then being suffered by the church, it was decided in 1904 to sell the ground. To save the building, however, it was moved to an adjoining plot, the church being lifted bodily by a hundred mine workers, put on to rollers and moved to its new site — and there re-established!

Not long afterwards, however, it proved too small for the growing congregation and a larger building became necessary, for which a fresh location was found.

Lord Milner, British High Commissioner, laid the foundation stone in March 1905 and the new church — the present building — was officially opened by his successor, Lord Selborne, in January the following year. Designed by the architects Simpson and La Gerche, it was built by Alexander Stuart and Company.

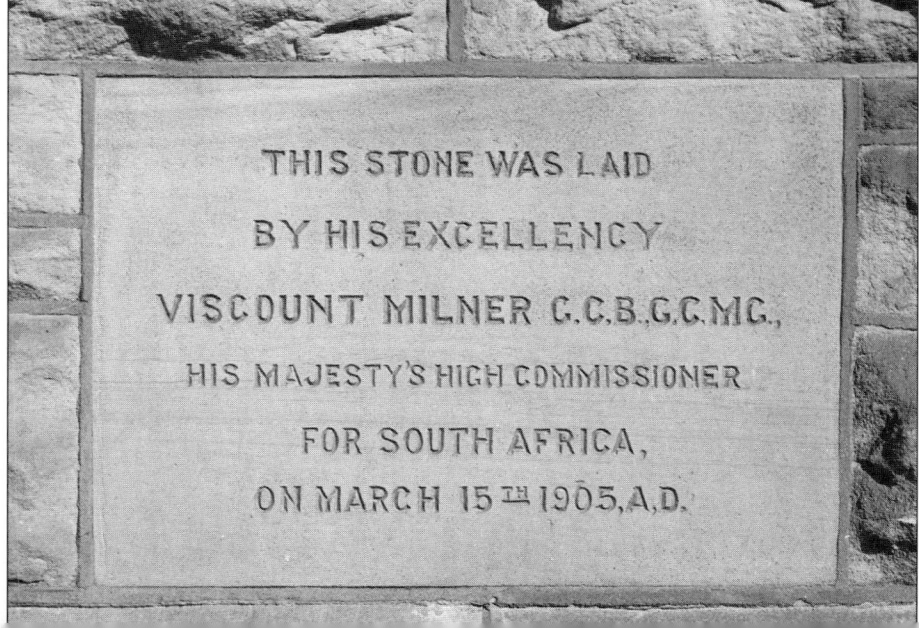

THIS STONE WAS LAID
BY HIS EXCELLENCY
VISCOUNT MILNER G.C.B.G.C.M.G.,
HIS MAJESTY'S HIGH COMMISSIONER
FOR SOUTH AFRICA,
ON MARCH 15TH 1905, A.D.

The church is neo-Gothic in style with a tower topped by a conical steeple that rises from a slender ornamented octagon which itself rests on a square red-brick base. A second tower, found to be unsafe, was removed some years ago. The gabled front is dominated by a fine rose window set into the façade which provides a splendid sight from across the street and down the length of another. The colourful brickwork is edged with white stucco moulding, which gives emphasis to the architectural lines of this interesting place of worship.

Through the double gates on the pavement, steps lead to a shallow porch with doors into the church on both sides. Functional stubby columns of black and white provide the frontage with relieving decoration.

139

*(Right)
Large adjacent
commercial buildings
now overshadow
the church*

The size of the octagonal interior is deceptive, its height making it appear larger than it really is. Far from being awesome in any way, however, the interior has great friendliness and a warmth that is enhanced by the splendour of the woodwork. Great dark beams from the eight corners curve to a meeting point in the centre of the dome-like ceiling. The gilded pipes of the large organ at the front, together with the light colour of the oak pews — arranged in arc formation facing the communion table and polished by more than a century of usage — give relief to the sombre sturdiness of the beams. Plain windows on the south side allow gentle light to the interior while the colours of several striking stained-glass windows in the north wall and in the gallery add warmth to this quiet place of prayer.

The days have long gone, alas, when St Andrew's Church stood proudly on its own. It is now hemmed in by large modern city buildings which, while emphasising that a place of worship is essentially a part of the community, tend to dwarf its majesty and conceal the gracefulness of its architecture.

Now a declared National Monument, St Andrew's in Germiston is a tribute to those early immigrants and their descendants who in that community have contributed so richly to the development of the country's wealth and progress.

Nederduitse Gereformeerde Kerk
Pretoria East

*(Left)
The Byzantine-style dome
and modified Gothic
tower of the Nederduitse
Gereformeerde Kerk
in Pretoria East*

Pretoria's metamorphosis in 1910 to being the Administrative Capital of the Union of South Africa led, inevitably, to a hastening of the town's growth and a proliferation of suburbs to accommodate the expansion.

As they matured, those suburbs themselves became social entities more and more independent of the town's core. In 1920 the Dutch Reformed community in Sunnyside to the east of the town's centre formally hived off from the Mother Church in central Pretoria and formed a congregation of its own — which, in turn, was later to divide into further separate parishes as the town grew.

Great tribute must be paid to the aesthetic foresight of the committee of church members responsible for the building of this new church. They had visited a number of parishes in the Transvaal and Free State in search of ideas for their building and, early in 1926, in their guidelines stipulated that "... the exterior shall not be the same as those of the stereotyped church buildings already built for many various church congregations..."

This brief exactly matched the ideas of a young architect, Gerard Moerdijk, keen to pioneer new architectural styles for South African churches —

*(Right)
Breaking with tradition, Moerdijk arranged the seating in an octagonal arena to face the pulpit*

styles that would take local conditions into account and also utilise local materials.

An initial building tender of 42 552 pounds by J. Coenen exceeded the funds available and adjustments had to be made. By using cement blocks instead of sandstone, by delaying the construction of the tower until further funds became available and by making certain other adjustments, the price was brought down to 37 352 pounds and construction work began early in 1927. The foundation stone was ceremonially laid in April of that year.

There was a certain unease — it is told — over the fact that a stately tower had become a victim of these economies, and it was suggested that the women of the parish should set about raising the necessary funds, the reward for which would be the placing of a hen instead of a cock as the weather vane at its summit!

The architecture of this attractive church reflects Moerdijk's ideas, drawing on a number of classical styles which, blended with skill, give it a significant yet harmonious character. Its Byzantine dome — with Etruscan tiles — does not clash, for example, with the well-proportioned Roman-style columns of the building, nor with its modified Gothic tower.

The bell in its tower was originally cast in Germany in 1887 for the church in Pretoria's central square which in 1904 was dismantled to settle a dispute between factions of the Dutch Reformed Church.

Moerdijk's new church was consecrated in May 1928. The organ — its construction delayed in Holland — was installed five months later, while only many years afterwards, in 1956, was a clock added to the tower.

Since then the complex has been enlarged by the addition of other buildings: there is now a large hall as well as modern administrative buildings close by, while lawns and gardens, shrubs and trees add to the overall attractiveness of the site.

It is not merely the external elegance of this church which makes it noteworthy, however. It has significance for its pioneering architectural role and the development of a design which has since

been used in several new Afrikaans churches throughout South Africa. Eschewing the earlier traditional cruciform, with parallel rows of pews in the nave at right-angles to those in the transepts, Moerdijk arranged the seating in an octagonal arena, with all the congregation directly — and comfortably — facing the pulpit.

In that sense this church is not only a place of worship, but also a monument to Gerard Moerdijk, a distinguished Afrikaner and an innovative architect of his times.

Opposite the church, beyond a tangle of intersecting streets, is Loftus Versfeld, headquarters of the Northern Transvaal Rugby Union. Through the years, hundreds of thousands of enthusiasts streaming to rugby games, however intent on rugby, could not have failed to notice this striking church. How many, one wonders, have given a second thought to its pioneering architectural role and to the achievements of the famous South African architect, Gerard Moerdijk, its designer.

(Above)
The entrance portico on the north-east side

The Zion Christian Church
Moria

(Right) The broad valley at Moria becomes a vast open-air place of worship for the masses of followers who attend the ZCC's Easter festivals

Of all the hundreds of independent churches in South Africa which, in one form or another, describe themselves as Zionist, the Zion Christian Church (ZCC) at Moria is both the largest and most significant. Today its members are counted in hundreds of thousands and the movement continues to draw large numbers of black Africans to its ranks. Its annual religious festival at Easter attracts millions of devotees from all over South Africa and neighbouring countries to its headquarters near Pietersburg in the northern Transvaal.

No single building could accommodate such masses, and the church at Moria — a large and plain yellow-painted edifice which elsewhere might pass as a warehouse — reckons its capacity in only a few hundred. But the Zion Christian Church, now split into two, possesses the whole of a broad valley which on these occasions becomes a vast open-air place of worship that conveniently accommodates the millions of religious visitors at festival time.

On the slopes of the hill across the valley, in a space cleared from the scrubby bush above the complex that is the headquarters of the movement, a large five-pointed star with the words "Zion City Moria" beneath it, is picked out in white-painted stones. The symbol can be seen from afar and serves as much to mark a place of worship as any Cross shining from a cathedral steeple.

The word "Moria", taken from the Book of Genesis, means "provided by the Lord".

This South African Zionist connection with the first Zionist baptisms by the American missionary, Bryant, at Wakkerstroom (q.v.) in 1904 can be traced through its development and a line of interlinking personalities. What came initially

from the United States as a white Christian movement was integrated from its start in South Africa with the baptising of whites and blacks together in the Snake River — seen in this context as the Africans' Jordan. Since then, some practices modified, segments have broken away and many — such as the ZCC — have become movements for black Africans only.

At a time when such segregation is breaking down in South Africa, a notice at the entrance to Zion City expressly forbidding "Europeans" to take photographs within its precincts strikes a strange note.

It has long been argued that the political situation in South Africa which precluded black participation in political movements channelled their desires for recognition into religion — one area in which some freedom was permitted in the segregated society. This concentrating of natural forces gave impetus to the development of religious organisations and enhanced the power of leaders deprived of authority in other spheres.

Among such men was Ignatius Lekganyane, from the Pedi tribe, who laboured and studied at a Zionist mission in Lesotho in the early 1920s before returning to South Africa and setting up his own Zion Christian Church in 1925 in the northern Transvaal. On his death in 1950, the church was taken over by his son Edward and, in due course, by Edward's son, Barnabas. The increasing size of the movement recently led to its division into two bodies, the second group led by Engennas Lekganyane, a cousin.

The creeds of both are the same: basically traditional Christian practices and beliefs to which some local innovations have been added.

On joining, besides re-affirming their commitment to Christian mores, members have to foreswear the use of tobacco, alcoholic drinks, drugs and certain foods.

Members of the respective groups are identified by their lapel badges: the group run by Barnabas has a ringed silver star with a green cloth tab as an emblem; while the other has a dove — bird of peace — similarly embellished.

Since adherence to the Zionist Church demands self-control and personal discipline, these badges of membership have become practical credentials for those seeking employment.

Leaders and senior officials of the movement have been criticised for their ownership of expensive motor cars and for their generally opulent manner of living, which leaves no doubt that the Zion Christian Church is indeed a wealthy organisation. Its leaders have considerable authority over their followers and, indirectly, that gives them a certain power — albeit vicariously, perhaps — in political affairs.

The charisma of the leaders is made obvious by the extraordinary attendance of millions of black Africans who flock to Moria for the annual Easter festival. To get there men, women and children travel by train, motor car, taxi, and buses by the hundred. They walk and ride, singly and with families, and, in their millions, camp in the open air in the bushy valley for three or four days, ignoring discomfort that is often exacerbated by heat and frequently by rain.

At that festival the religious services are relayed by radio and by line from the small yellow church on the side of the hill, the words and music booming across the countryside from hundreds of loudspeakers fixed to poles in the valley.

On the fringes vendors capitalise on basic needs — foods of all sorts and, among other items, water sold in large plastic bottles for drinking and to be blessed.

The scene each year is richly colourful. And perhaps unique. For those few days the entire valley becomes a vibrant open-air place of worship, resounding to prayers and praise in the adoration of their God.

The Greek Orthodox Church
Pretoria

(Above) The dome gives national character to this Greek church in Pretoria

Had Alexander the Great's plans to circumnavigate Africa not been nullified by his untimely death in 323 BC, Greeks might have been among the first navigators from the northern hemisphere to set foot upon the shores of southern Africa. As it was, however, modern history tells us that the first Greeks to settle in the country were three sailors who jumped ship in 1880 and began farming in the eastern Cape, inland and away from the sea. In recent years, however, migration has been brisk and more formalised and many thousands of Greeks have settled in this country, taking on South African nationality but at the same time — with understandable pride — retaining links with their historic culture as well as maintaining their traditional religion.

The number of Greek schools and churches in some of the bigger cities indicates the force of that pride in their heritage. None retains its Hellenistic character more, perhaps, than the Greek Orthodox Church in Hatfield in Pretoria, where, in the fabric of the building, traditional Byzantine designs have been modernised and adapted to the climatic conditions of South Africa.

The main characteristic of classic Byzantine architecture is the dome, a feature dating from the fourth century when builders in the eastern Mediterranean developed the means of placing a circular overhead construction upon a rectangular base without a central support.

In AD 330 Constantinople, formerly Byzantium and now named Istanbul, a city founded by Greeks, was made the capital of the ruling Roman Empire shortly after Emperor Constantine had established Christianity as the state religion. In the circumstances it was inevitable that, in the development of the new capital, churches were incorporated in plans accommodating the new

religion. Their construction came under the influence of local custom and, more and more, the basilica design of Roman Europe came to be replaced by the styles of the East. At the same time, Roman construction techniques were absorbed by Byzantine craftsmen. Two centuries later this cross-fertilisation of styles and methods reached its high-water mark in the magnificence of the monumental Hagia Sophia, the supreme masterpiece of Byzantine architecture. With the Ottoman conquest in 1453 it became a Moslem mosque, and minarets were added.

From the sixth century and for the next 400 years, political wrangling between East and West, accompanied by differences in religious matters, culminated in the splitting of the Christian Church; the two parts being controlled by Rome and Constantinople respectively. The schism influenced the architecture of later places of worship.

The Greek Church of Eastern Europe clung to its established orthodox doctrines and looked to Constantinople for inspiration, maintaining the individualistic domed Byzantine style of architecture. Western church architecture, following European styles, continued with the classic basilica plan.

Traditionally decoration in churches had embraced statuary and the portrayal of people and animals. Emperor Leo III (717-741) in Constantinople, however, fearing that this would lead to idolatry and paganism, banned the representations of human and animal forms in places of worship. Protest led later to an amendment of this decree and while sculptural representations of such subjects continued to be outlawed in Eastern Christian churches, painted figures became permissible. The ban on statues was not observed in Western churches which, after the schism, were controlled from Rome.

Through succeeding centuries the respective traditions have been generally maintained. Whereas statues are to be seen in most Roman Catholic churches — and, to a lesser degree, in other Western Christian churches — decoration in Greek orthodox churches tends to be limited to painting. In the Greek church in Pretoria decoration takes the form of some fine painted icons, though wooden saints and angels carved in Athens are represented in bas-relief form.

Many of those icons form a part of a screen behind which, in Orthodox churches, the altar is located — unlike the design of many other churches where the altar is set in full view of the congregation.

This Greek Church in Pretoria is an impressive building, made even more striking by the unusual nature of its design and appearance. Designed by the Johannesburg architect May von Langenau, it is set in large grounds in Hatfield, with a large community hall at hand. The broad classic dome, painted red, is topped by a large Cross. The main entrance is through a portico supported by plain concrete pillars, the hard edges of the rectangular porch being softened by the curves of the arches between the pillars. This church building combines traditional form with contemporary construction.

Inside, the building is light and airy, the high ceiling and the depth of the dome above a broad concourse creating a sense of great spaciousness. With the gallery above the main entrance at the back, there is accommodation for a thousand worshippers. This modern place of worship breaks with tradition in providing seats for its congregation; classically, worshippers stand in Orthodox churches.

The foundation stone of this Greek church was laid in August 1969 by Pope Nicolaos VI, Patriarch of Alexandria, who returned to South Africa in June 1972 also to bless and formally inaugurate the church.

The church lives as a chapter in continuing ecclesiastical history and brings to South Africa a lively symbol of the long-established Orthodox Christian religion as well as something of traditional Greek church art and architecture.

(Above left) A gilded icon flanked by carved angels inside the church

(Above) The magnificent sanctuary screen decorated with Greek-style icons

Nederduitse Gereformeerde Kerk
Lydenburg

(Above) The present church with the historic old church building in the foreground

Something of the history and the development of the Dutch Reformed congregation in Lydenburg in the eastern Transvaal is made manifest in its old church buildings. There are two, close together, while across the street is the small old schoolhouse, also a National Monument, which in early times was used for church services. The school building is no longer in use, however; it remains quietly proud simply to be the oldest school building in the Transvaal. The original church building today also stands locked and empty, silent in the shadow of its tall, handsome successor.

But as much as their fabric tells of the growth in the numbers who worshipped there through the decades, these buildings tell little or nothing of the rest of the fascinating history of the town where, to an unusual degree, the religion and the politics of the community were closely linked.

While the first congregation and the first church across the Vaal River were established at Potchefstroom (q.v.) in 1842, Lydenburg, further north and considerably more remote, was the third community in the Transvaal to build a church — a few months after Rustenburg.

The name Lydenburg — "Town of Suffering" — was given by the first settlers there, Voortrekkers under Hendrik Potgieter who had undergone tribulations in their search for a permanent home. Firstly, chased north of the twenty-fifth parallel by the widening net of British legislative authority,

*(Left)
The magnificent carved pulpit, copied from that in the Moederkerk in Stellenbosch*

they established themselves in the north-eastern Transvaal and named the place Andries-Ohrigstad after their leader and a benevolent Dutch merchant, George Ohrig.

The march of seasons, however, showed the area not to be well-disposed to settlement. Summer rains brought the scourge of malaria and death to numbers of Potgieter's party. This led the Trekkers to seek another home and, in 1849, abandoning Andries-Ohrigstad, they moved about 50 kilometres southwards to higher ground, safe from malaria. There they created a fresh settlement which they named Lydenburg as a memorial to those who had died and, too, as a tribute to the sufferings of those still living who had endured the bitter anguish of earlier hardships.

On the day following the fixing of the new site in January 1850, one of the Trekkers, Antoon Fick, petitioned for the erection of a building in which the small community might "practise the religion". A supporting subscription list showed that 59 people had promised to contribute 525 Rix-dollars, eight wooden beams and a dozen planks, each 12 metres in length, towards its construction.

It is remarkable that while dwellings were humble in those days of early settlement, each village had a substantial church built by communal effort even though there was very often no fulltime minister.

Building of the Dutch Reformed Church went ahead despite the absence of any minister, the village school teacher, Master Poen, conducting the services. When the Reverend Andrew Murray and the Reverend J.H. Neethling from the Cape paid a visit to the congregation early in 1852, the little church, though not completed, was given a temporary roof of reeds for the occasion. An encircling wall was added later to enable the building to be used as a fort if necessary.

Completed in the following year, this church served the community for four decades until, in 1889, when the congregation had grown too big for this building, it was decided to erect a larger place of worship. The Reverend Neethling laid the cornerstone on 12 April 1890 and the church was consecrated almost exactly four years later.

The builder was J.H. Parker. The final cost, slightly exceeding the original tender price, amounted to some 12 119 pounds.

In those four decades the smaller church building had witnessed a number of nagging church problems, however: problems in which the politics of the infant Transvaal Republic became interwoven with doctrinal policies of the church.

Firstly, in 1853 the congregations at Potchefstroom and Rustenburg asserted their independence by refusing to be incorporated into the Cape Synod. Despite the decision of the General Assembly of the church in the Transvaal, Lydenburg took a different line and, adhering to the Synod at the Cape, seceded from the newly formed Transvaal church organisation, turning a deaf ear to pleas to unite with that body.

At much the same time unity among the Transvaal churches was made impossible by a liturgical dispute concerning the singing of hymns at services, and the congregation at Rustenberg, led by Paul Kruger, broke away to form a free Reformed Church. It was held that because hymns, unlike psalms, were not a constituent element of the Bible, they should not be a part of the service.

*(Right)
A plaque expressing gratitude for the inauguration of the Bible in Afrikaans*

Not only did Lydenburg decline to join the Church Assembly of the Transvaal, but in February 1858 it also declared itself politically independent of the rest of the Transvaal by becoming an independent republic, later to join with Utrecht in a political union which lasted from May 1858 until the coalition joined the Transvaal Republic in 1860.

Lydenburg's links with the Moederkerk at Stellenbosch influenced aspects of the design and the interior of its new church in the 1890s.

While the name of the builder — J.H. Parker — is known, the name of the architect is uncertain. The close resemblance of the design to that of the Witkerk in Middelburg (q.v.), not far away, leads to the thought that Lydenburg's church may well have been influenced by the Witkerk.

The Witkerk was designed by Carl Otto Hager, a well-known architect of that time. Its foundation stone was laid three years prior to that in Lydenburg, so it must have been under construction when Lydenburg decided to build its new church. Links between the two towns were close; indeed, Middelburg was a creation of the Lydenburg Republic when, in 1859, the Republic wanted a resting place half-way along the road to Pretoria, and Middelburg — the "middle-town" — was established.

The two churches have many stylistic similarities. Both are cruciform in style; both have similar gallery structures, windows of the same shape and style, pews which are very much alike, and beams, roof trusses and wooden ceilings which are not dissimilar. In both, the magnificently carved and beautiful wooden pulpits — neo-Gothic in style and with similar aspects of design — are the outstanding decorative features of their interiors.

The building commission wished the pulpit in the new church at Lydenburg to be a replica of that in the Moederkerk at Stellenbosch, and to ensure that this was done the carpenter, Palframan, and his assistant, De Roo, were sent to the Cape to study the pulpit there. The result is magnificent. Made from kiaat donated by Abel Erasmus and grown on his farm north of Lydenburg, it is a fine work of noble proportions. Hooded and standing tall, its elegance is enhanced by the delicate hand-carved motifs and scrolls.

Through the years the building has required certain renovations. These have been done with commendable care, ensuring that the character of the building has not been spoilt. For example, when the original oil-lamps were replaced by gas-lamps which, with the march of the years, were superseded in turn by electric lights, the style of the lamps was carefully maintained and the character of the church respected.

This church and, indeed, the historic complex of churches and the school today stand as fine memorials to the past in an area now made prosperous by the mineral wealth of this region.

The Mariaman Temple
Pretoria

(Below)
The splendidly ornamental gopirum *of the Mariaman temple in Pretoria*

The recently built westbound highway from the centre of Pretoria skirts the precincts of the old Tamil temple at Marabastad, erstwhile Indian quarter of the city, allowing passers-by now to catch a glimpse of this remarkable building with its tall *gopirum*, an ornate gateway.

It is this unusual structure which catches the eye and, indeed, visually so dominates the part of the temple behind it that few sightseers bother to examine the rest of the picturesque and interesting building beyond the entrance.

None would contest the statement by experts that "This is the most impressive *gopirum* among Hindu buildings in South Africa". Without question it is uniquely significant in the country's Hindu culture, contributing richly to the diversity of the nation's heritage.

The construction of this sacred place, dedicated to the goddess Mariaman, took several years. Begun in 1927 on the site of an earlier, simple wood-and-iron temple, the building was completed only 11 years later, a solid structure of brick and stone and cement. It stood then in the centre of the Indian quarter of Pretoria, its *gopirum* reaching proudly above the surrounding houses as tradition demands, for custom insists that the temple gateway should always be the highest and most visible structure in a communal area — constantly reminding a Hindu of his continuing religious responsibilities and, too, at all times providing an entrance for the spirit in search of salvation.

The *gopirum* was added later, after the main part of the temple had been completed. Designed by Govindasany Krishna, born in South Africa, and assisted by another Indian, Govender, the gateway was erected under their supervision by a local builder named Van Vuuren. The size and proportions of the building, as well the types of materials used, followed strict traditional rules of building; rules that were laid down millennia ago and passed on from one generation to another, firstly by word of mouth and then, from about AD 500, in detailed texts — the *Mansara* and the *Silpa Sastra* — which dictated not only how Hindu temples should be built, but also how Hindus should design their houses and lay out their towns and roads.

In the establishment of those rules a variety of factors were taken into account. Originally they not only included such matters as the location of the temple within a community, but also dealt with the relative heights, widths and breadths of its structure. The rules took into account, too, astrological factors which stipulated the calendar time for commencement of the work. While many of the details of those calculations seem to have disappeared, or now to be overlooked, the basic

rules remain known and continue to be observed in the construction of Hindu religious buildings.

In India, centuries ago, the interpretation of these rules was influenced by the availability of local materials and through the ages two distinct styles developed. Most of the Indians who migrated to Natal in the final decades of the nineteenth century came from the south and brought with them the Dravidian type of architecture which prevailed there.

This style is distinguished by its emphasis on horizontal characteristics in the design, whereas the Nagara architecture of the north tends to focus on vertical delineation in the structure of its religious and community buildings.

Certainly the emphasis on horizontal characteristics in Pretoria's Mariaman temple makes plain its links with southern India. The façade of the *gopirum* consists of horizontal tiers, one above another, decorated with encircling bands of fascinating mythological figures cast in concrete. The domed top of the structure, 12,5 metres in height, is decorated with seven *kalasas*, symbolic sacred flames of life, indicating the sacred nature of the building they adorn.

These intriguing concrete figures on the façade were cast in South Africa, using moulds brought from India.

In Marabastad the *gopirum* stands close to the street, protected by a low fence of iron railings with a double gate in front of two heavy doors. The

(Above) *Details of some of the ornamentation, in Dravidian horizontal style, on the* gopirum

ornate, towering concrete gateway, broad at the base, has its own places of worship within. Beyond is the main concourse, the *mandapam*, centre of the temple, open on three sides and with the traditional pool of water to remind worshippers of the essential need for cleanliness of body and mind during devotions.

Between the *mandapam* and the *gopirum* is the *kodi*, a tall pole with three beams at its top, horizontal like a flag in a stiff breeze. Its base is set in a symbolic navel depicted by a lotus with an indentation at its centre. The *kodi* symbolises the male reproductive organ and the strength of the god, while the horizontal beams represent the three earthly elements — water, fire and air.

On the fourth side of the central area is another room, glassed in and smaller in size, with three deep recesses — the most sacred area of the temple. Here are placed representations of the temple gods themselves. In the centre niche, set slightly further back than those flanking it, is Mariaman, the main deity of this temple. One of seven goddesses in the Hindu pantheon, she represents the malevolent aspects of the character of Shiva, whose consort she is. It is to appease her maliciousness that offerings are made to her and a low table before her is usually laden with gifts of fruit.

From the recess on her right, a brightly dressed representation of Ganesa, a son of the great god, Shiva, looks out through the archway into the centre of the temple. He has the head of an elephant on a plump, well-fed human body, his head and trunk in this representation being of shiny brass. He too is worshipped since traditionally it is Ganesa who clears away obstacles which might frustrate contact between the worshipper and god.

In the niche on Mariaman's left is a brightly clad representation of Muruga, god of war and god of power. Traditionally he is accompanied by a peacock, which remains always close to him and is regarded as Muruga's vehicle. It is the peacock which carries the worshipper on his heavenly journey.

Some years ago, political strictures in South Africa led to the transference of the Indian community from Marabastad to Laudium, some distance away. While this temple was not forgotten nor did its functions cease, it ceased to be the centre of the Tamil community in Pretoria. But its historical and cultural significance could not be overlooked and callous moves to demolish it were frustrated by its being declared a National Monument.

In 1991 the temple underwent restoration and remains now an interesting part of the nation's cultural heritage, available for study and to be reverently enjoyed by all who care to visit it.

(Far left) *The inner sanctum of the temple*

Nederduitse Gereformeerde Kerk
Middelburg

(Right) The venerable "Witkerk" in the centre of Middelburg

There was a strong biblical ring to the early name given to the little settlement where, mid-way on their slow, dusty journeys between Pretoria and Lydenburg, transport riders with their ox-wagons in the latter half of the nineteenth century used to outspan and rest.

The settlement was founded and developed to provide such a facility and in 1866 was formally named Nazareth, though — inevitably perhaps — its location had earlier led the site to be referred to descriptively as Middelburg.

At the same time it was decided to build a church there and the congregation dates its establishment from the following year, though for some years services were held in a makeshift church — which had to be extended in 1877 — while money was being raised to build a permanent place of worship.

As it turned out, this delay was perhaps not without many advantages. By the time the decision was taken in January 1888 to proceed with the building of a new and larger church, the council was able to gauge the size of the enlarged community and to arrange capacity accordingly.

The new place of worship — thought to have been designed by the well-known church architect, C.O. Hager, and built by his son — was consecrated on Saturday, 18 January 1890, notwithstanding the fact that building was not totally completed. Everything was ready except that the interior of the impressive tower had yet to be plastered and was awaiting the installation of the bell and the clock, ordered from Germany, which had not yet arrived.

The week-end of the consecration was given over to the celebration of the traditional *Nagmaal* — Holy Communion — and provided an opportunity for the baptism of numbers of children of farmers who, in the custom of those times, had come from the outlying areas in their tented ox-wagons and camped around the church for the days of the celebrations.

With the establishment of this fine new building in the town's centre, the previous church together with the adjacent grounds were sold and the money was used to reduce the debt incurred in the erection of the larger church.

During the Anglo-Boer War the British established a large military camp close to Middelburg, accommodating some 30 300 troops, and the Dutch Reformed church was used by the army on Sunday mornings after the congregation's own services, a practice of which many villagers did not approve.

(Above left)
The beautifully carved pulpit with its Gothic-style canopy

(Above)
The early sunshine warms the tower of this well-known old Transvaal place of worship

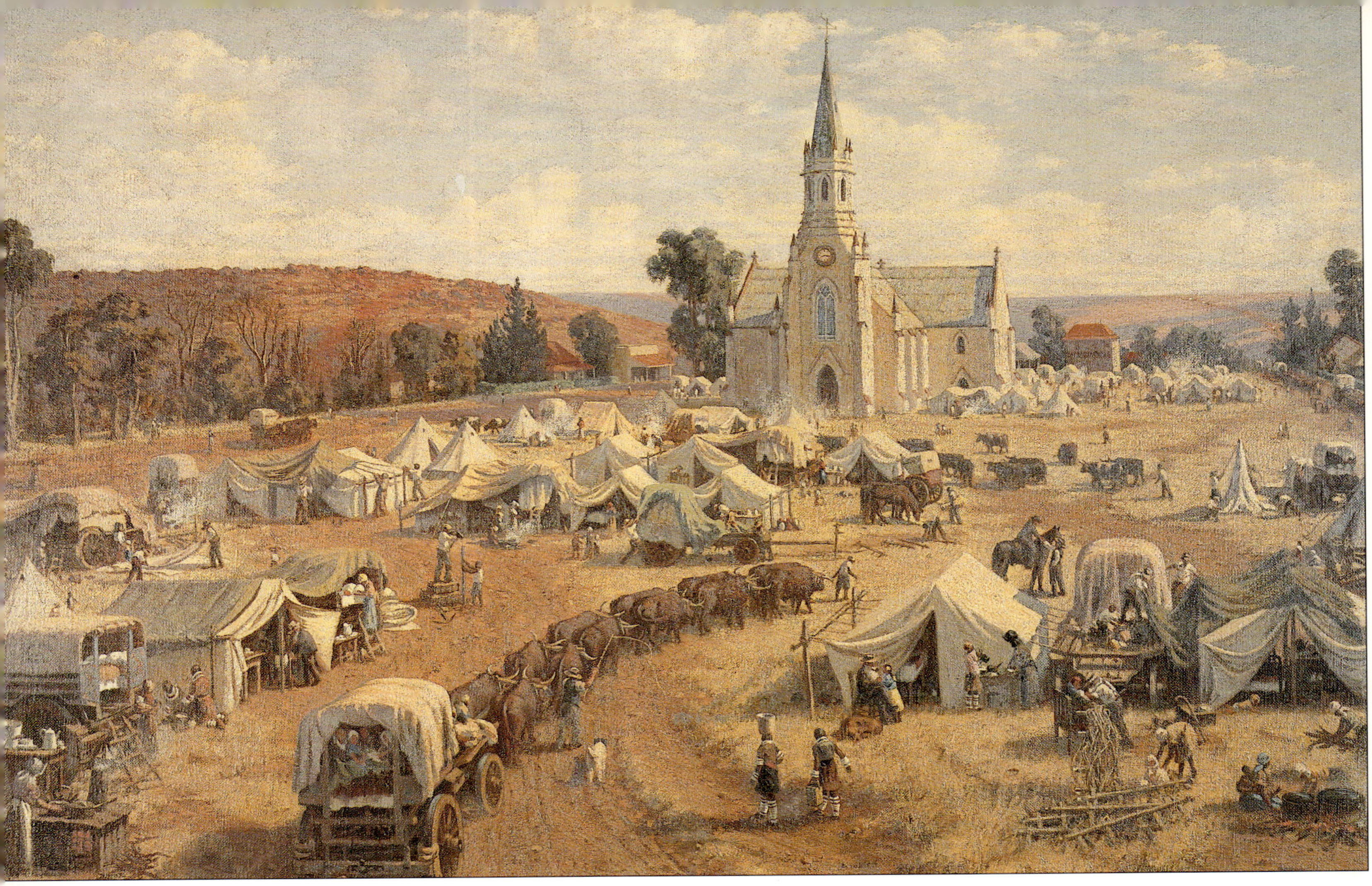

(Above) *Willem Coetzer's historic painting (1938) of* Nagmaal *at the church in the nineteenth century*

This church at Middelburg — popularly known as the "Witkerk" — is attractive and interesting, both for its history and its architecture: a large white cruciform building in extensive grounds made colourful by flower beds. Above the rectangular porch, the clock tower is extended by a tall conical steeple rising from a small drum. The bell with tinkling sound gives notice of the passing hours, its voice, designed to be heard by the hamlet's small community, is too gentle now to be heard over today's enlarged town and across the surrounding rolling hills.

It is the beauty of the church's interior, however, which compels attention, with its graceful, curved wooden beams, the wooden ceiling and the colours of the timber in the panelling of the galleries. The pulpit is magnificent. Grand in its concept and structure, delicate in its carving, this pulpit, with a curved stairway on each side, has a steepled Gothic-style wooden canopy above it, supported by delicate columns, and decorated by sharply pointed pinnacles which further lead the eye upwards. Carvings on the base add to the decorative effect and emphasise the delicate lightness of the structure.

A painting by Willem Coetzer, the well-known South African artist, of *Nagmaal* at the Witkerk sometime towards the end of the nineteenth century shows the broad open space around the church filled with tents and wagons, people and animals, depicted very realistically, in the golden glow of a tranquil late afternoon in autumn.

How times have changed! No longer are there extensive open spaces around Middelburg's historic Witkerk; the needs of a developing town have absorbed the ground. No longer do families get together for several days to celebrate *Nagmaal*. The community spirit, deriving from ties with the church, is different now. Today farmers come to church by motor car and, after an hour or two, return home. But changed circumstances have done nothing to alter the essential spiritual role which the church continues to play in the community and of which the Witkerk continues to be a part.

WITKERK

HIERDIE KERKGEBOU HET DIE OORSPRONKLIKE GRASDAKKERKIE VERVANG VAN DIE NED. GEREF. GEMEENTE NAZARETH (NOU MIDDELBURG) WAT OP 9 MAART 1867 GESTIG IS. DIE HUIDIGE GEBOU IS WAARSKYNLIK DEUR DIE BEKENDE KERKARGITEK, C.O. HAGER, ONTWERP EN IS IN 1890 DEUR SY SEUN, J. C. M. HAGER, VOLTOOI. DIT IS EEN VAN DIE OUDSTE BESTAANDE NED. GEREF. KERKGEBOUE IN TRANSVAAL.

Geproklameer 1984 Proclaimed

THIS CHURCH REPLACED THE ORIGINAL THATCHED CHURCH OF THE NAZARETH (NOW MIDDELBURG) DUTCH REFORMED CONGREGATION, FOUNDED ON 9 MARCH 1867. THE PRESENT BUILDING WAS PROBABLY DESIGNED BY THE WELL-KNOWN CHURCH ARCHITECT C. O. HAGER AND WAS COMPLETED BY HIS SON, J.C.M. HAGER, IN 1890. IT IS ONE OF THE OLDEST EXISTING DUTCH REFORMED CHURCHES IN THE TRANSVAAL.

Raad vir Nasionale Gedenkwaardighede
National Monuments Council

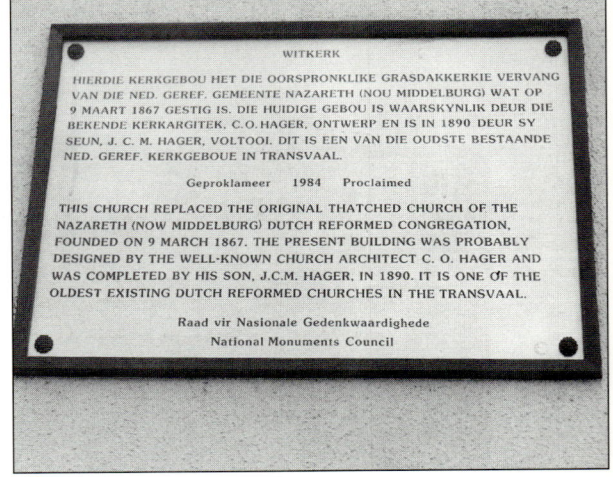

(Right) *A National Monuments Council plaque records something of the history of this church*

The Lion *Shul*
Johannesburg

(Left) The well-loved old Lion Shul in Doornfontein

An article in the London Jewish Chronicle of 16 March 1906 describing the recently built synagogue in Doornfontein, Johannesburg, said that, "... Though small, the new synagogue is exceedingly pretty — perhaps, in its structure and scheme of colouring, the most beautiful in South Africa...."

While — inevitably — personal preferences and judgements lead to a continuing debate as to which is indeed the most beautiful synagogue in the land, it is common cause that this place of Jewish worship — the oldest in Johannesburg — in a very changed, modern and developing Doornfontein, certainly remains one of the three or four most attractive gems of all synagogues in South Africa.

It was built in 1905 to serve the Doornfontein Hebrew Congregation, which was established in the previous year and which consisted primarily of English and German Jews who, after the Anglo-Boer war, had moved to the new suburb of Doornfontein, described in the London Jewish Chronicle at the time as "one of the prettiest residential quarters of the town." Though the character of the suburb has changed considerably since then and not many Jews now live in the area, the synagogue is still regularly used.

The architect was M.J. Harris, son of an English Rabbi, Mark Harris, and the first Jewish architect on the Witwatersrand. The cost of the building amounted to some 4 000 pounds, considerably exceeding the architect's original estimate of 2 500 pounds. The foundation stone was laid on 18 August 1905 by Sir Arthur Lawley, KCMG, Lieutenant-Governor of the Transvaal, and the synagogue was officially opened on the same day.

Like so many suburbs, Doornfontein, once the main and fashionable Jewish residential area of Johannesburg, has had its ups and downs. At present it is fast becoming a business area and this historic synagogue risks being dwarfed and overwhelmed by larger and taller buildings in a concrete jungle.

As a result of a severe fire which in the 1930s considerably damaged the structure, the synagogue underwent major restoration and a certain amount of rebuilding, which altered the appearance of the original building.

(Left)
An unusual painted glass window setting out the Ten Commandments in Hebrew

Today it is a grey-fronted building, the steps and the columns at the entrance at its western end on busy Siemert Street guarded by two large black-painted cast-iron lions — with staring yellow eyes — sitting upright at the bases of two lamp-poles. It is these striking ornaments which give the synagogue its popular name: the Lion *Shul*.

In its architecture, the exterior of the synagogue is a mixture of oriental and Western styles, with octagonal domed minarets reaching above a façade with classical Western-style columns.

Three doors with windows decorated with the Star of David, recessed beneath curved arches supported on stubby half-columns, lead into a shallow entrance hall which has stairs on both sides leading to the women's galleries that overlook the main concourse of the synagogue on three sides.

The galleries are supported by well-proportioned marble columns that continue upwards to the high ceiling which features three shallow domes of mottled glass. Besides admitting light into the main hall, these domes also provide ventilation. Further light is provided through plain windows in the side walls above and beneath the galleries.

Above the Ark, set in an apse at the eastern end of the hall, is a striking stained-glass window with the Ten Commandments set out in Hebrew in black script on clear glass between strips of red, blue and yellow. A large golden Star of David in a circle adorns the centre of an arched triptych at the top of the window. No record of the origins of this window can be traced.

In the mid-1950s land was purchased on the northern side of the *Shul* and a Talmud Torah built there to serve the Jewish community. The decision failed to take account, however, of the fact that the Jewish population of the area was then moving from Doornfontein and it was not long before the school closed down. The building remains nevertheless, leased to a business concern.

At a time when so many links with the past are having to make way for newer buildings, one hopes that the Lion *Shul*, significant both in an architectural and historical sense, will remain — an impressive souvenir of Doornfontein's earlier more illustrious days and of Johannesburg's historic past.

(Left)
One of the cast-iron lions guarding the entrance to the synagogue — giving the popular name to this place of worship

The Lutheran Mission
Botshabelo

(Above)
A view of Botshabelo mission from the Wilhelm (now Merensky) Fort on the hill behind the church

About 12 kilometres north of Middelburg in the Transvaal, on the road to Loskop Dam, lies the old Berlin mission station of Botshabelo, established in 1865 by two young German missionaries, Heinrich Grutzner and Alexander Merensky. The latter's son, Hans, born at Botshabelo, years later carved a niche for himself in South African history by his remarkable geological discoveries in the eastern Transvaal. Set in a wooded valley, Botshabelo is hidden from the road. It is only the modern-style Ndebele-painted gateway which indicates that anything of interest lies beyond.

Though no longer actively a mission station, Botshabelo retains much of its quiet charm and character implicit in the name given to it by Merensky — meaning "Place of Shelter".

Here there are two churches: both interesting. But it is their history rather than their architecture which merits consideration, though certainly their construction evokes admiration for

the pioneers who built them. The older, of plastered brick on a dressed-stone base, is now a museum. It could perhaps be mistaken for a Victorian office building were it not for the small bell-turret over its main doorway and the crosses prominent at the apexes of the twin gables on its eastern side.

Attention to the other church, however, yields greater rewards.

This simple red-brick building, which might perhaps be described as "modified Gothic", is set on the hillside overlooking the farm and the mission buildings below. Its angular brick tower and pointed spire reach up from the thatched roof and, seen from afar, the spire appears to be floating on the bushy green of the tree-tops as it pokes through the foliage of the surrounding oaks and poplars and the indigenous bush of the hillside.

The extent to which this place of worship has been used over the decades is made manifest by the worn state of the hard stone steps. Untold thousands of feet — some shod, many bare — have climbed those steps to worship.

Outside this unpretentious country church, quiet and remote from the bustle and noise of urban traffic, traces of confetti in the crevices of the rutted, stony pathway tell how popular this chapel continues to be for weddings.

Construction began in 1868, when, three years after Merensky and Grutzner had bought this large farm, it was found that the first church there could no longer accommodate the burgeoning congregation. They had paid 500 Prussian talers (about R150) for the 3 000 hectares of farm land which embraces large open grazing areas as well as a deep valley and ravines worn by the rivers of many millennia. After more than three years, the little church was completed and consecrated. Later it was enlarged by the addition of transept wings, making it the cruciform structure it is today.

The original construction required 300 000 bricks, each one being hand-made and then baked in the hot sunshine. The rafters and much of the woodwork within the church were sawn from yellowwood brought by ox-wagon from Pongola, while the plain Gothic-style windows are decorated at their apexes with simple designs in stained glass which were fashioned at Botshabelo from materials imported from Europe.

The dung floor enhances the feeling of the history and the simple rusticity of the place,

(left)
Steps trodden by thousands of worshippers climbing to the mission church

(Right)
The site of Botshabelo in the nineteenth century

*(Far left above)
The first church at the mission is now used as offices and to house a small museum*

*(Left)
The plain interior of this simple mission church*

recalling the life and customs of those pioneering ancestors who explored and opened up the wide, sweeping lands of our country.

Quickly after its foundation the settlement became self-sufficient. The farm provided meat and vegetables, while grain was ground at the mission's own water-powered mill to provide flour.

But life at the mission was not always peaceful.

Availing himself of the sanctuary which this Christian mission offered, one of Chief Sekukuni's brothers sought refuge at Botshabelo with a number of his followers. Angered by this and by the inroads which the missionaries were making upon his tribe and his authority, Sekukuni attacked the mission. This led Merensky to build a large fort at the top of the hill overlooking the tiny settlement. Here the inhabitants of Botshabelo took refuge when necessary, driving their animals into large stone-walled kraals attached to the fort which Merensky named after Emperor Wilhelm of Germany.

From its sturdy crenellated tower one gains a splendid view across the farmstead below and the *vlaktes* of the encircling game reserve; a magnificent panorama reaching to the far horizons.

Later the fort was used by British troops in the Anglo-Boer wars of 1880-81 and 1899-1902.

Across the river there is now an Ndebele settlement, the walls of the neat mud huts in the village bright with the colourful designs and picturesque patterns for which that African tribe has become so well known.

Further up the valley are the old cemeteries, marked by low dry-stone walls, the graves now overgrown by tall grass and Africa's tropical vegetation, too vigorous to contain, too copious to control. For those who care to pause and read, the headstones have much history to relate, many tales silently to tell. Troops of monkeys scamper through the tall grass and swing through the sunlit trees in the green valley that is Botshabelo — the Place of Shelter.

The Zionist Church
Wakkerstroom

Travellers in rural South Africa grow accustomed to finding the Dutch Reformed Church situated in the epicentre of the towns — and in this respect Wakkerstroom is no exception. Built of local sandstone, the church dominates the little town, its tall tower to be seen from far across the surrounding flats and beyond the river and from the gentle hills which ring the wide, grassy plain all around.

It was built in 1888 to replace an earlier church which had grown too small for the congregation which dates its establishment from 1861.

Wakkerstroom — its name, "Lively Stream", taken from the character of the river there — is one of the older settlements in the south-eastern Transvaal. Proclaimed a township in 1859, through the years it has served as the centre of a prosperous agricultural area and this church has been the focal point of worship for the community.

But as prominent as that church is, historically its fame is eclipsed by a religious movement which had its South African origins in Wakkerstroom and which, in its diversity, has now burgeoned and spread throughout the land to become the biggest and most populous religious movement in southern Africa.

No monument of stone, nor of bricks and mortar marks its beginnings there, however. Reeds in the river itself and the lonely grass on its unattended banks, down beside the old abandoned road bridge, now grow and die with the passing seasons on the unmarked spot where the rites of this new movement were first seen in South Africa; a historical ceremony destined to inaugurate a new era in Christian practices throughout the land and to establish a fresh religious denomination whose influence has since spread far beyond the boundaries of South Africa.

It was here, in what was then called Snake River, that on 24 May 1904 Dr Daniel Bryant, an American Zionist missionary, baptised not only a number of whites but at the same time also made history by conducting the first Zion baptism for blacks in South Africa.

Among the whites then baptised were P.L. Le Roux and his wife, both of whom were ordained by Bryant a few months later as an elder and an evangelist, respectively, in the Christian Catholic Church in Zion which had its origins in the United States.

Petrus Louis le Roux had studied under the great Andrew Murray at the Missionary Seminary at Wellington in the Cape and, as a missionary in the Dutch Reformed Church, had been sent in 1893 to Wakkerstroom on the Transvaal-Natal border to work among the Zulus.

His views on a number of issues were at

(Above) *The old bridge beside which the American, Dr Daniel Bryant, performed the first Zionist baptisms in South Africa in 1904*

variance with those held by the Dutch Reformed Church — especially on matters of faith healing and the baptism of infants — and Le Roux resigned to join the Zionist movement in March 1903, working closely with Bryant from his base at Wakkerstroom where he instituted the first Zulu Zion.

Le Roux once worshipped in the honey-coloured stone Dutch Reformed Church which still stands in the centre of the town. Travellers speeding over the large modern concrete bridge on the edge of the town hardly notice the old bridge, not far upstream, identifying the place where Le Roux, amid controversy, was baptised and where Zionism had its beginnings in South Africa. For millions of South Africans that river is now their River Jordan. Its grassy bank was their church — their place of worship. Open to the sun and the air, the sky is its ceiling. The wind and the water give it music and the changing colours of nature provide its decoration; eyes look to the watching hills from which the soul gains help and strength — as the Psalmist tells.

Little could Bryant have known, at the time of those first baptisms in the Snake River at Wakkerstroom, that before the end of the century the Zionist movement would have spawned the largest church community in southern Africa.

So large has it become that it has split into two groups which have their headquarters side by side in a wide valley at Moria (q.v.) in the northern Transvaal. The church building on a hillside overlooking that valley is far too small to accommodate the millions of worshippers who gather in prayer to celebrate the resurrection of Christ.

For three or four days every Easter millions of African Zionist worshippers camp peacefully in that valley, overlooked by ancient hills which similarly bring them help and strength.

(Left) *The present Dutch Reformed Church in the centre of Wakkerstroom*

Universiteitsoord
Pretoria

While the location of the Universiteitsoord Dutch Reformed Church in the midst of the rapidly expanding University of Pretoria makes this modern church a finite part of student life, it remains independent of the university itself — unlike the chapels and churches of older European universities and colleges such as those of Oxford and Cambridge, for example.

With a congregation that swells and subsides substantially with the tides of the quarterly academic terms, the architects and planners were faced with the problem of ensuring adequate space for a large congregation during term-time and, no less, also eliminating the spectre of a sea of empty pews when, during vacations, most of the students have dispersed.

The problem posed an unusual architectural challenge: how to devise a means of providing flexibility of capacity without impairing the corporate unity of the interior as a whole.

This challenge has been skilfully met by dividing the seating area into various levels. The main seating, in front, is supplemented by a gallery with rows of pews sloping upwards from those on the ground floor. This large and separate upper section is split yet again by a narrow balcony and, when required, its higher area can be completely shut off by a heavy curtain, mechanically operated.

Beneath the gallery is a large open entrance hall which can be utilised when necessary to accommodate an additional 500 people simply by adding the required number of extra chairs. The overall range of flexibility — between 500 and 2 000 worshippers at any time — thus admirably solves the problem created by the nature of this church's particularly itinerant community.

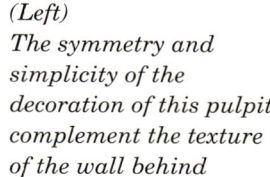

(Far left above)
The southern aspect of the Universiteitsoord church in Pretoria

(Left)
The symmetry and simplicity of the decoration of this pulpit complement the texture of the wall behind

(Left)
The cross-section of the church illustrates the flexibility of capacity inherent in its design

(Far left below)
The pipes of the organ, together with the dalles-de-verre window by Leo Theron, provide an ornamental pattern on the northern wall of this place of worship

(Left)
The graceful tower at the western end of the church is a feature of the surrounding area

(Right)
Mr F. W. de Klerk being sworn in as State President by the Chief Justice of South Africa, the Honourable Mr Justice Michael Corbett, September 1989

Its useful size and capacity — doubtless coupled with the simple dignity of the building — made the Universiteitsoord Church an appropriate venue for the swearing-in of Mr F.W. de Klerk as South Africa's State President in September 1989, almost exactly 24 years after a former State President, C.R. Swart, had formally laid its foundation stone.

A tall white pulpit of hammered concrete is the focus of attention within the liturgical area. In relief on its front is a monogram made up of the Greek letters X and P, meaning "Christ is King", a symbol used first by Christ himself and later, in the year 325, selected as an emblem by Emperor Constantine the Great.

To assist in providing optimum acoustics, sound engineers of the Council for Scientific and Industrial Research were consulted in the planning stages and the pulpit was scientifically positioned in accordance with the requirements of the internal shape of the building. A fibre-glass sound reflector was later suspended above the pulpit to project the preacher's voice to the congregation, especially to those worshippers seated beneath the gallery.

Among the most attractive features of this building are the unusual texture of the brickwork and the fact that there is not a sharp rectangular corner in the whole edifice. Each brick was split in half and laid with its rough edge outwards. The walls were reinforced internally with a further layer of bricks and, to ensure complete strength, sections of the walls are tied to stout concrete pillars in the framework.

The roof, which at its west end sweeps proudly upwards in a magnificent, soaring tower, more than 30 metres high, follows the ancient architectural basilica formation with three sections: a classical high centre above the nave, with lower side roofs above what in earlier churches would have been aisles. The clerestory windows between the higher centre section and the side roofs allow ample natural daylight into the building, diffusing the light throughout the spacious interior.

On the side walls of the liturgical area are two floor-to-ceiling windows in the *dalles-de-verre* style: small panes of thick glass set in concrete, their colours, carefully selected and arranged by the artist, Leo Theron, making variegated patterns of the intruding sunshine.

The 3 022 gilt pipes of the large organ — built in South Africa — are set in rhythmical groups of varying sizes on the north wall near the front of the church, adding ornamentation to the interior as a whole.

To enter, one crosses an open-air, brick-paved forecourt at the eastern end, a modernised conception of the classical atrium which traditionally formed an integral part of the ancient basilica. A bronze plaque set in the centre of the paving pays tribute to the parents of members of the congregation whose contributions helped to build the present church.

The architect was Jan van Wijk, himself a graduate of Pretoria University.

The harmonious lines and construction of this architecturally interesting church contribute to the beauty of Hatfield where it is situated. The sweep of its soaring bell-tower, seen from far and wide, especially adds majesty to the proliferating campus of the University of Pretoria.

Rhema Church
Randburg

(Above)
The new chapel of the Rhema church in Randburg

The Rhema movement which began in the United States is a part of the current explosion of Christianity that has led to a proliferation of independent charismatic churches which have spread, under various names, into many parts of the world.

The word "Rhema" (pronounced *rayma*) is derived from Greek and can be translated as "the spoken word".

In substance, if not in formal affiliation today, the Rhema movement at the outset would seem to have close links with Pentecostalism which developed in North America in the first decade of this century and which has developed remarkably since then, leading to a number of parallel movements that have spread rapidly throughout the Christian world. Pentecostalism is regarded as the world's fastest growing Christian movement today.

In the pursuit of Christianity, its basic beliefs lie in baptism by total immersion, in healing by faith and also in "speaking in tongues" — that is, when seized by the Spirit of God, as a manifestation of faith, believers speak words which often have no meaning known to man.

The international headquarters of the Rhema movement are in Tulsa in Oklahoma. There the Rhema Bible Training Centre accepts students for training in divinity and eventual ordination as pastors.

It was here that a young Ray McCauley from Johannesburg, after his studies and ordination, received a divine message to return to South Africa and there to found a church.

He obeyed. The large, modern church complex in Randburg is the visible manifestation of its success since the beginnings of the movement in South Africa in 1979.

But that edifice was not created overnight. Nor did the acceptance of the movement come about without travail. Beginnings were small, but growth quickly snowballed, and the series of meeting

168

(Left)
The clean lines of the new and modern church in the Rhema complex

places grew in capacity one after another to accommodate the growing congregation.

Today the auditorium at the Rhema church is the largest meeting hall in South Africa. It seats 5 500 people and twice on every Sunday morning more than two-thirds of those seats are filled. Attendance at an "overflow" service each Sunday evening averages between 3 000 and 4 000 worshippers.

The large complex of buildings, elegantly modern, has a commanding position on a hillside above the spacious grounds necessary to provide parking space for the thousands of worshippers. High on the façade of the administrative building the word "Rhema", in bold letters, is accompanied by the crest of the movement — the word "Faith" in the form of a shield and sword.

The complex was designed by a Johannesburg architect, Gorwyn O'Neill.

The buildings look across acres of well-kept lawns with a variety of shrubs, as well as a small decorative lake beside some trees which break up and soften the view of repetitive rows of parking spaces.

On the north side of the large main building is a chapel, newly built for use when the vastness of the auditorium becomes too overwhelming for a particular occasion. It seats 400. The buildings of the Bible Training Centre occupy the other flank of the administration block. It takes in 450 students at a time on a two-year diploma course. A video and television centre not only provides videos worldwide to take the teachings of Christ into thousands of homes, but also provides material for broadcasting, thus bringing those teachings to thousands of families in many countries.

For the Rhema Church music has been — and is — a very vital and important component in its development. In the auditorium as well as in the chapel the traditional church organ has been replaced by a modern bandstand, with state-of-the-art electronic sound equipment and performing space for a large band of musicians with electric guitars, percussion instruments, as well as the latest in brass and keyboard instruments. In its style the music here may be said to be closer to the Beatles than to Bach!

These services aim to bring Christianity to the people and to show that it is a joyous way of life, rather than something to be endured in one's Sunday best once a week.

Rhema is a member of the South African branch of the International Fellowship of Christian Churches (IFCC), a loose federation of charismatic churches founded in 1985 and now with a membership of over 500 churches and 400 000 Christians throughout the country.

The amazing growth of Rhema is a further manifestation of the substantial religious revival currently being experienced in South Africa and may be said to demonstrate a growing need among people — now better educated — not only for a renewal of traditional faith but also for an updating in the practice of everyday Christianity.

(Far left)
The stage and modern interior of the chapel

An Interdenominational Chapel
Verwoerdburg

*(Right)
The tiny private
red-brick chapel
of meditation beside
the man-made lake
at Verwoerdburg*

(Left)
A stained-glass roundel in the chapel, the white dove symbolising peace

Beside the man-made lake and tucked quietly among towering modern office buildings in Verwoerdburg is a little, elegant, newly built (1991) red-brick chapel open to all who, amid the bustle of the day's labour and the strains and stresses of life, need moments of solitude and a sanctuary for meditation and peaceful prayer: a place where pace yields to peace.

Its situation is reminiscent of many of those historic little churches in the cities of Europe; old buildings which once stood alone and which have now been enveloped in the town's growth. But, of course, this chapel at Verwoerdburg is different. It is not an old church which has been absorbed in the course of urban expansion, engulfed by enterprises of a later age, but is one purposefully placed amid contemporary buildings to be a part of the ongoing growth and development of a massive business complex.

It is heartwarming, in an era of brash commercialism, to find space allocated in a progressive commercial centre for a building which yields no monetary returns, but which in human terms brings rewards rich beyond tangible limits.

For Christians such purposeful respect for their God in the midst of their daily labours may be seen to indicate freedom from enslavement to money, recalling the biblical admonitions of both Saint Matthew and Saint Luke who, despite the ridicule of the money-loving Pharisee merchants, warned that man cannot serve two masters: he cannot be the slave of both God and money.

It is a small, well-proportioned chapel, measuring only 3,4 by 5,2 metres internally, with seating for 12 people. The floor is tiled. Strong beams support the steeply pitched ceiling, while the roof hangs low on either side, shielding from hail the windows of blue and golden-yellow panes, with the gold depicting a Cross in the centre of the window. Above the entrance is a tall tower, hollow inside, topped by a pitched roof which gives the building a Germanic appearance.

There is no altar. A simple lectern stands in a shallow recess at the front, ornamental glass bricks on either side of the alcove allowing nature's soft light to illuminate this important front area of the chapel.

High above the front alcove is a colourful stained-glass roundel, designed and made by a local artist, featuring a white dove that epitomises the inner spiritual peace and peacefulness to which this sanctuary is dedicated.

The idea of this unusual chapel originated with a group of Christians inspired to contribute something to the daily life of the community and who insist on remaining anonymous. The initiative and enterprise of those who originated this scheme were backed by the local authorities.

The fact that this place of worship has been given no name and has not been dedicated to any specific saint or denomination crystallises the wish to keep it available to all who desire the benison of that tranquillity which yields spiritual comfort to those who sincerely and quietly seek it.

174 The Tweetoringkerk
Bloemfontein

178 St Patrick's Cathedral
Kroonstad

181 St Augustine Mission
Modderpoort

184 Nederduitse Gereformeerde Kerk
Winburg

187 The Berlin Mission
Bethany

190 Nederduitse Gereformeerde Kerk
Senekal

193 Our Lady of the Assumption
Qwa Qwa

195 Nederduitse Gereformeerde Kerk
Kroonstad

(Facing page)

*The entrance to the cave chapel
in the rocky Platberg at Modderpoort*

Orange Free State

The Tweetoringkerk
Bloemfontein

(Right)
A view of the back of the Tweetoringkerk

Though not the only twin-towered church in the country, this Dutch Reformed Church in Bloemfontein is known throughout South Africa simply as the Tweetoringkerk. Perhaps it earned this sobriquet to distinguish it from the many other churches in the city; but, more probably, it stemmed from affection and from the important role it has played in the development of Afrikanerdom throughout the country.

Church towers serve many purposes. In simplest terms, they help to distinguish a place of worship from the buildings around it, adding to the architectural character which people have been conditioned to associate with established places of worship, be they Christian churches, Moslem mosques, or of any other religion. Certainly, towers draw the gaze upwards, taking the human spirit with them into the infinity of the heavens from where the gods of many faiths watch over their believers on earth. In open country the towers of village churches stand out as proud landmarks, beacons for the traveller, as symbols of community, offering friendship and comfort to strangers. In practical terms, too, church towers raise the bells above their earthbound surroundings, allowing their calls to ring out unimpeded across the neighbourhood and surrounding countryside. Often too in times of hostility church towers have been used in the protection of the local community — as look-outs for watchers on guard against attack.

Some towers are square in design, others rounded. Some are plain, others are ornate. The variations in design are infinite, often making their particular faiths manifest by their styles, and in the decoration embellishing them.

But the predecessors of this church in Bloemfontein did not always have two towers. In fact, the first — erected on the site where the Tweetoringkerk now stands — was a plain and simple edifice without any tower at all. It was the first church in Bloemfontein, its cornerstone laid by the British Resident, Major Warden, in January 1849.

But while its congregation was the first in Bloemfontein, it was not the first church community to be founded north of the Orange River. Winburg (q.v.) was established seven years earlier, while Fauresmith was next. But, of them all, Bloemfontein was the only church community which then had a minister of its own — the young Andrew Murray, who took up his calling there in 1849, shortly before his twenty-first birthday, and who went on to contribute so much to the Dutch Reformed Church in South Africa.

That first church building served the community well for more than 20 years when, with

the growth of the town and the congregation, a larger building became necessary. It was decided to demolish the old building and to erect a new one on the same site.

President Brand laid its cornerstone on 10 May 1878 and construction went ahead rapidly under the supervision of R. Wocke, the contractor. Two years later, the building was formally consecrated with considerable ceremony. Its twin towers are said to have been modelled on the eleventh century cathedral of Bamberg in Bavaria.

These towers stood proudly through years of domestic strife as well as through times of war elsewhere in which South Africans fought. Quietly too they witnessed important changes in the political structure of the country, in the course of which Bloemfontein became one of the three capital cities of the new nation and the location of the highest court in the land.

All was well until, suddenly, one night in April 1935, almost 60 years after its erection, the western tower collapsed without warning, destroying the clock and causing considerable damage to the rest of the building. The other tower cracked and threatened also to fall, before it was quickly dismantled. Only the bases of the towers remained, level with the roof.

Fortunately no lives were lost in the disaster, but the absence of the towers became sorely felt — not only by the congregation itself, but also by the citizens of Bloemfontein who grieved the loss of a well-known and well-loved landmark, which had become a part of the very ethos of the city itself.

Indeed, so much had those towers become established landmarks that it was felt the church could not continue without them and the congregation set about repairing the omission. Renovations were carried out as soon as funds had been raised, and a number of other alterations were also effected, including the installation of a new organ. These reparations were completed towards the end of 1942, but it was not until June 1950 that, thanks to the generosity of the City Council, there was again a clock in the western tower of the Tweetoringkerk.

The years resumed their gentle flow until January 1952, when their calm was again suddenly interrupted by tragedy.

One night vandals broke into the building, set fire to the beautiful and historic old pulpit and damaged the organ. The mahogany pulpit, magnificently hand-carved by Ernst Schmidt, was destroyed completely: senseless destruction. In the course of the repairs, a new and larger pulpit replaced the lost work of art: behind it now is the new organ, with a handsome gallery built around it.

The beauty of the interior of the Tweetoringkerk springs from its symmetry and simplicity: it is almost austere in its plainness. The church is cruciform in design, with aisles flanking the central block of pews of light-coloured wood. The woodwork is adorned only by the patina of age and

(Far left)
The broad pulpit and impressive organ gallery

(Left)
Items in the church's fine collection of silver

usage. Stout beams with small squared capitals support the fine wooden gallery on three sides. The windows are plain, relieving ornamentation being limited to patterned arrangements of rosettes of uncoloured glass.

The organ gallery and the cluster of silvered organ pipes provide a majestic backdrop to the broad wooden pulpit that extends across the front of the nave.

Various memorial plaques decorate the porch; vignettes of history, echoes of the stilled voices of great personalities. They are not limited to South Africans alone, however. One, a white marble plaque, is a memorial to "Nederlanders en Oud Nederlanders gevallen voor de Republieken in den Oorlog 1899-1902." Among the names recorded there is that of C.V. van Gogh, who died of fever near Brandfort. He was a brother of Vincent, the famous nineteenth century Dutch post-impressionist artist. (There is a similar plaque at the Dutch Reformed Church in Du Toit Street in Pretoria.)

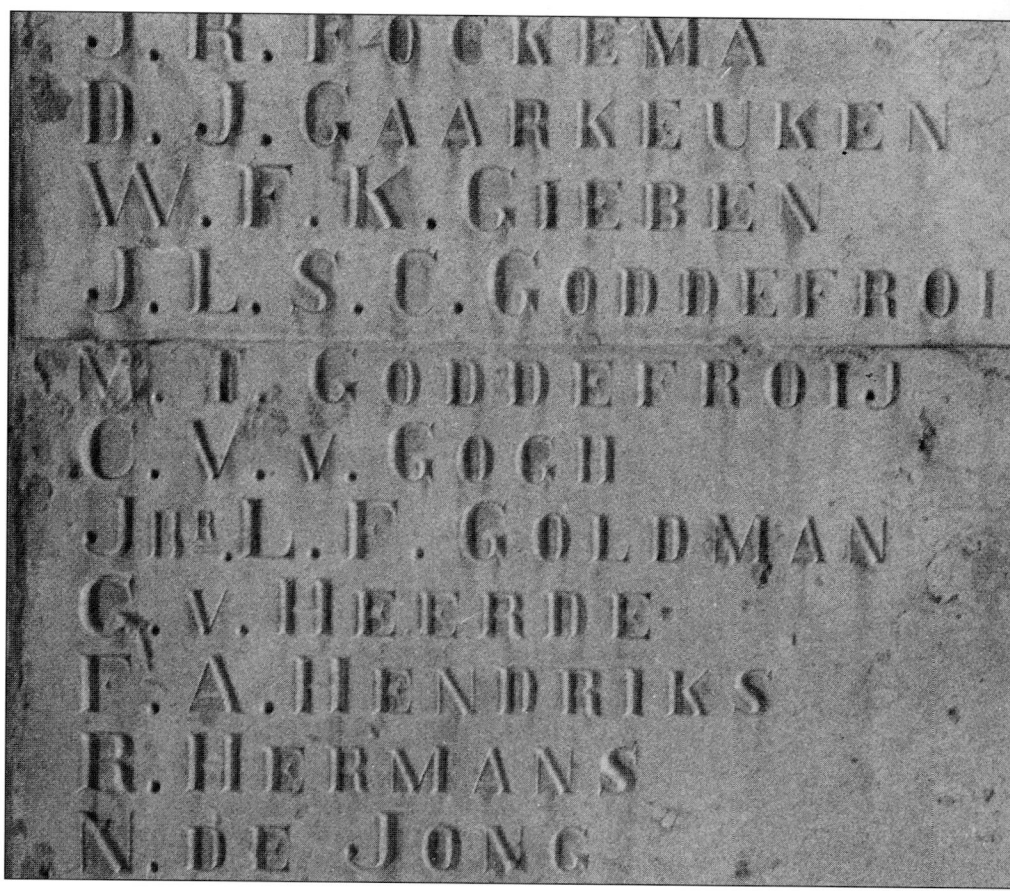

(Right)
Part of the plaque in the front entrance of the church showing the name of C. V. van Gogh — brother of the famous Dutch artist — who died in South Africa

177

St Patrick's Cathedral
Kroonstad

Kroonstad is well endowed with places of worship. One, at least, is the work of the well-known Till family of architects. But, for all the considerable attraction and interest of those others, perhaps the relatively new and innovative Roman Catholic Cathedral of the Resurrection takes pride of place.

Architecturally it is an unusual building. Its frontage is long and low, epitomising the flat landscape of the Free State, the façade a simple grille of white stone relieved at intervals by thin columns. No soaring spire seeks to mark the church from afar. Instead, a simple Cross surmounts the low dome rising from a flat roof like a lone koppie on the wide veld.

Dedicated to St Patrick, perhaps because it replaced the old cathedral built by Irish soldiers after the Anglo-Boer War, the new cathedral is innovative not only in its external appearance, but also in its square interior where the elevating of the area of worship on to a single plane at once unites the congregation with the officiating priest — in keeping with current liturgical trends.

The altar is large: a single block of stone brought forward towards the worshippers, thus further contributing to the union of worshipper and officiant.

The ceiling is low, but the quality of natural lighting which floods through the clerestory windows on four sides gives an impression of added height. Of plain glass, these windows are saved from starkness by a decorative metal grille.

But if this South African place of worship ignores some of the established and more ornate architectural traditions of older cathedrals in Europe, its art follows earlier classical traditions by using the skills of the best available contemporary artists in the adornment of its precincts.

The most prominent of the art works is the large black-and-white mural — nearly 20 metres wide — across almost the entire wall behind the altar. It is the work of the well-known South African artist Cecil Skotnes, and executed in an unusual technique — sgraffito — in which a base of black plaster is overlaid by white plaster into which the design is then engraved.

Its theme is that of the Resurrection. Here man's place in the Resurrection is depicted as the prodigal son, who loses his way and then finds it again through Jesus himself. Abraham and Moses symbolise early biblical events, while the dynamic centre of the mural illustrates the Crucifixion and, between Christ crucified and the depiction of the final coming of God's Son, man himself is seen waiting.

Here the Stations of the Cross, to be seen in every Roman Catholic church, have also been illustrated by Skotnes. He veers away from the usual mode of illustration, however, and presents

(Far left)
The front of St Patrick's Cathedral, low and flat, in keeping with the surrounding countryside

(Left)
The Sixth Station of the Cross in a series by Cecil Skotnes. Veronica wipes Christ's face as He stumbles on His walk to Golgotha

(Left)
Barbara Greig's representation in terracotta of the Resurrection of Christ, in the chapel of the Blessed Sacrament at the Cathedral

179

(Above) Detail from the large mural by Cecil Skotnes behind the altar

the classical episodes in a dynamic series of fine individualistic woodcuts.

Above the altar of the small adjacent Chapel of the Blessed Sacrament, to the right of the cathedral's main entrance, is a magnificent frieze by Barbara Greig representing the Resurrection of Christ and his meeting with the 11 disciples in Jerusalem. Thomas is seen set apart from the others, to the right of Christ. Adorning a plain, whitewashed wall this frieze in terracotta is lit by natural light from a skilfully concealed window above, emphasising the relief of the modelling of the sombre-coloured figures.

Ten small colourful *dalles-de-verre* windows, designed by Elizabeth Sebok and made by Whitefriars Studio in England, bring warmth to the chapel.

In the cool, soft light of the Baptistry, on the other side of the cathedral, a fine allegorical painting by the South African artist, Maud Sumner, symbolises man's necessary link with Christ to fulfil the promise of Redemption. The creation of such a link by the act of baptism makes it fitting that this painting should be installed in the Baptistry.

The spirit of Resurrection is emphasised also by a tall decorative bronze statue of the Archangel Gabriel, the work of Zoltan Borboreki. Its size is lost in the perspective of his position high on a tall and narrow metal plinth on which he stands above one corner of the cathedral building — his trumpet ready to announce the Second Coming of Christ.

The inspiration and skills of a Johannesburg architect, Jan van Gemert, conceived the design of this cathedral, incorporating current liturgical trends to meet the common needs of priest and people, blending tradition and innovation and using available local art to beautify a place of worship that fits comfortably into the environment which encompasses it.

St Augustine Mission
Modderpoort

(Below)
The entrance to the unusual cave church at Modderpoort

Modderpoort is not a very felicitous name for any place, least of all an attractive part of the eastern Orange Free State which deserves a happier description. The "Muddy Defile" is that between the free-standing Viervoetberg and the low Platberg, an extended flat-topped mountain feature, as its name describes.

The region has been inhabited for millennia. Old Bushman paintings were found in caves of the area in 1820 as were several Stone Age artefacts, while records indicate that the poort was used before the waves of Trekkers swept northwards across those plains and began to open up the southern African hinterland.

How it came to be a religious centre in the nineteenth century is interesting.

In his struggle against the Zulus, Moshesh, chief of the Basotho, sought the help of the Europeans, then seeping into the area from the south, and sent cattle to buy two missionaries of the Paris Evangelical Society to serve his people. Though the cattle were stolen by marauding Griquas on the way to being delivered, the missionaries responded to his plea, averring that the Word of God could not — and should not — be bought with worldly goods. Those French Protestant missionaries arrived at Modderpoort in June 1833, but soon moved to Morija, the first missionaries to enter Basutoland (now Lesotho).

In the late 1860s the Anglican Bishop of Bloemfontein, Dr Edward Twells, purchased two large farms in the Modderpoort area for the purpose of establishing a church mission station to serve the eastern Free State and Basutoland.

To implement the scheme, in 1867 he founded the Society of Saint Augustine, the first indigenous Anglican religious society on the continent of Africa, and the first such Order to have its origins and roots in South Africa. It was named after Augustine, the great early Christian theologian, influential writer and teacher, who laboured in north Africa where, at the end of the fourth century, he became Bishop of Hippo in what is now Algeria.

Appointed as head of the newly established missionary brotherhood, Canon Beckett, with a handful of devoted young Englishmen, arrived at Modderpoort in 1867 and set about the tasks of constructing buildings, tilling fields for food and developing a mission station, while, at the same time, working to spread Christianity over the vast area allocated to them as their missionary responsibility.

While living quarters were being built, they lived, worked and prayed in a rocky cave on the lower slopes of the Platberg.

*(Above)
The altar inside the cave church*

Canon Beckett described the situation in a letter written soon after his arrival there in April 1869: "... On Saturday, after unloading... we turned our attention to the ordering of a cave, in which we have made our temporary abode. By building up a wall of stone we have contrived to enlarge the area, so as to get a room, twelve feet by fourteen, for a chapel, beside a small sleeping room... Both rooms we have much improved by digging away the floors, so that I can now stand upright in the chapel, and *sit* upright in the bedroom..."

With these pioneers came an English stonemason, W.J. Terry, who had volunteered his services to the brotherhood for three years. The fine sturdy buildings of honey-coloured, dressed stone stand yet at Modderpoort, a memorial to his skills, his labours and his dedication.

The cave on the slopes of the Platberg is still used as a chapel. Dim-lit, plain and rough within, it is preserved as a monument to those early devoted and dedicated members of the St Augustine brotherhood who founded the mission station. They built well. Now they rest in peace in the quiet, shady cemetery on the hillside. To the north of the cave, on the higher slopes of the Platberg, a larger stone church was built, dedicated to Saint Augustine. Three fine stained-glass windows, designed and made by the English artist, Kempe, in 1889, decorate the east wall above the altar. One of these depicts Saint Augustine on Christ's right hand — indicative of the high regard in which this scholarly theologian is held among Christians.

Without a base in England, however, from which to draw fresh recruits, the Order of Saint Augustine slowly shrivelled and became unable to maintain the mission station which it had initiated and developed.

In 1902, an appeal for help was made to the Society of the Sacred Mission (SSM) in Britain, and new life was breathed into the mission at Modderpoort by the arrival of brothers from that Order.

Modderpoort became — and remains — the headquarters of the Society in southern Africa.

A Seminary was established to train men for the Christian priesthood and a college for higher religious studies followed. A High School and Teachers' Training College flourished for more than a quarter of a century — until closed down by political decree in 1955 when the mission's small cottage hospital was similarly compelled to cease work.

Today the large property is run mainly as a farming venture, supervised by a member of the

SSM. A conference centre is widely used, attracting people for meditation, discussion and prayer in the quiet of its environment.

The priory buildings on the guardian slopes of the Platberg look out across the broad plains below, each morning catching the early light of the sun rising from behind the far Maluti mountains, dwarfed by distance on the eastern horizon. Modderpoort is a place of beauty, belying the impression of its name; a place of tranquillity, warmed afresh each morning by a new day's light that banishes darkness and brings fresh hope, peace and a new spirit to that quiet corner of this troubled world.

(Below) African worshippers hold a service outside the cave church

Nederduitse Gereformeerde Kerk
Winburg

The handsome Dutch Reformed Church which presides over the large town square in Winburg stands as a proud monument to those courageous Voortrekkers who, in the first half of the nineteenth century, wound their difficult way northwards from the Cape to open up the interior of South Africa.

While several mission stations had been established across the Orange River prior to the coming of the main stream of Trekkers, and numbers of Europeans were already farming on lands beyond the border of the Cape, Winburg was the first town founded north of the Orange River, its establishment being formally recognised in 1842. The congregation was the first beyond the Cape borders, followed, across the Vaal in 1842, by the setting up of a Dutch Reformed congregation at Potchefstroom.

Both fell under the aegis of the first Voortrekker State, the short-lived Republic of Natalia, which embraced five widely dispersed church communities, over which Dr Daniel Lindley presided from Pietermaritzburg. Visiting Winburg in 1842, he set up the church's first Council there, and the congregation's foundation dates formally from that year. Dominee Dirk van Velden, a Belgian, became its first permanent pastor, taking up his post in December 1850.

A natural consequence of this appointment was the building of a church and a move was soon made to erect such a building. Dr Andrew Murray formally laid the cornerstone in 1853. For more than 40 years it served the community before becoming too small for the growing congregation.

John Henry Till and his cousin, A.E. Till, two English architects, were commissioned to design a larger church, and in September 1898, the tender of Messrs Rundle, Rowe and Marshall was accepted and building commenced. It was the year when the railway line reached Winburg. President Steyn laid the foundation stone in the following January.

The Anglo-Boer War interrupted construction, however, and then post-war depression led to further delays. For a while there was a reluctance to continue with the building.

It was the Reverend J.J.T. Marquard, the much respected Moderator of the Dutch Reformed Church of the Free State and the incumbent at Winburg, who, "against much pessimistic advice", persuaded the *Kerkraad* to complete the building, which was consecrated in 1904.

Feelings still ran high in the community and technical problems which compelled the builders to strengthen the foundations with additional cement — not least to sustain the weight of the tall and heavy stone tower — led a local citizen to remark

The Berlin Mission
Bethany

(Above)
Bare winter trees allow a view of the Berlin mission church at Bethany

From the Great North Road the low line of koppies is almost invisible across the infinite *vlaktes* of the Orange Free State. Winding west from the highway a lonely road crosses a railway line, seldom used, for trains seem reluctant to disturb the calm of those broad treeless grasslands, green in summer and golden in the dry winter sunshine. On and on for several dusty miles — and then suddenly a modest sign points shyly to Bethany, the historic mission which those rocky koppies conceal and protect.

The condition of the buildings, walled in, reveals at once that they are old. But the pervading dilapidation has been brought about not by the ravages of time so much as by usage; by the inevitable restless energy of hundreds of children who have been to school there through the passing decades.

Thousands of feet have trampled those playgrounds, making it difficult for grass to survive and easy for the red earth to turn to dust.

On a raised platform of rocks is the slogan "Education is the key", picked out in white pebbles to inspire the young African pupils who, from their appearance, are clearly from several different tribes.

The mission owes its foundation to the Berlin Missionary Society. In 1834 the mission obtained a grant of 12 square miles of land from Adam Kok, the Griqua chief of that area, and missionaries established themselves around a spring of perennial water beside these koppies.

There were innumerable problems and difficulties in those early years and, for a variety of reasons, the missionaries soon left. In due course the abandoned tasks were taken over by another German, Wuras, who laboured at Bethany for 50 years. His inspired work among the Korannas and Bechuana there set the mission on its feet and he is regarded as its real founder. In their teachings the missionaries had to use three alien languages — Dutch, Namaqua and Sechuana.

*(Facing page)
This tree, of which only a stump remains, was probably planted by those whose graves it later shaded before it, too, succumbed to old age*

*(Right)
Beside the altar, below the inscription, is the beautifully carved pulpit*

The church itself is plain and simple with a red iron roof. Its ochre-coloured plastered walls are built of square bricks brought from Germany! The windows are simplified Gothic in style, with small latticed panes of plain glass set in wooden frames. Quaintly, at the base of each old window is a small copper tube to drain water accumulated from the condensation of worshippers' breath in winter — a modification necessary during services in Europe's moist and snowy season!

The large church bell hangs from a free-standing frame of heavy timber balks outside and serves the mission school too.

The church interior, with its high ceiling, is no less plain: attractive in its somewhat monochrome simplicity. Around the arch of the alcove above the small altar is a quotation from the Bible, painted in quiet colour in Old German script. A gallery at the back overlooks the wooden pews of the main nave.

Undoubtedly the most beautiful feature is the tall, magnificently carved pulpit with panels of different woods and stairs reaching up to its entrance.

The old graves near the church in the lonely cemetery tell something of the hardship and the endeavour of those who pioneered the mission's existence here beside a God-given spring amid the remote koppies.

The founders themselves are buried beneath the trees in a separate section of the cemetery, the graves now overrun by creepers and threatened by the encroaching bush. The implacable veld has invaded the old communal cemetery so that only the tops of the taller memorial stones remain visible above the high grass which ripples in the wind as the veld changes from green to gold and back again, on and on through the hushed silence of the passing years.

*(Right)
Graves in the founders' cemetery*

Nederduitse Gereformeerde Kerk
Senekal

(Right) Prehistoric fossils decorate the low walls around Senekal's Dutch Reformed Church

As in most of the country towns in South Africa, the Dutch Reformed Church in Senekal is prominently situated on a large piece of open ground in the heart of the town, plainly visible from the roads which converge upon the square from all directions. Its presence is further emphasised by its silver-topped tower, rising above the encircling shops and offices on the outer perimeter of the square.

This site is enclosed by walls, rough-plastered and low enough to enable passers-by to enjoy the sight of the well-kept lawns and neat gardens around the old stone church. Decorative wrought-iron gates on each side give access to the building and the gardens.

Ned church was built in local rough-hewn sandstone towards the end of the last century, replacing a smaller church erected on the same site in 1875. A foundation stone set into the north-east corner tells that it was laid by James Collins, the *Landdrost* (Magistrate) of Winburg district, on 6 July 1895. A further incised inscription recalls the words of Verse 2 of Psalm 29, paying tribute to God and to "the splendour of His name".

The architects responsible for its design were the cousins J.H. and A.E. Till, who designed a number of churches in the Orange Free State and the Transvaal. A commemorative stone set into the front wall of this church in Senekal records their names as well as those of the *Bouwmeesters*, Rowe, Marshall and Hill, inscribed above a biblical reference to Nehemiah's rebuilding of Jerusalem.

A few years ago, the interior was renovated and today the beams of the high roof are supported by metal pillars encased in timber, while most of the front wall, behind the wide wooden pulpit, is

(Below)
Modern timber panelling within the church echoes the prehistoric connection with trees in the region and emphasises the biblical theme of the church gardens

(Below)
The tower of honey-coloured sandstone

decoratively panelled in ribbed light wood, the strips being used to provide a quiet pattern that relieves the extensive woodwork of wearisome plainness.

The sharp angularity of the centre panel of this modern-styled reredos — somewhat art deco — is softened by sweeping curves on either side, arcs which draw the eye back to the centre and which, with the dynamic line of the triangular middle panels, lead a worshipper's vision and thoughts upwards in praise and holy adoration.

The surrounding lawns and gardens cushion the church from intruding sounds: an oasis of quietude in a desert of pedestrian bustle. Monuments honour the founders of the town. There in the gardens, too, the flowers and shrubs, bushes and trees also carry the quiet messages of the Bible. It is an unusual and interesting place where the plants cultivated all have biblical links. Each is marked by a small plaque bearing its botanical name and with a note about its use, telling where a reference to it can be found in the Bible.

For example, beside a myrtle bush — *Myrtus communis* — stands a neat metal plaque telling that the leaves, finely ground and mixed with oil, may be used to soothe chafed skin. The myrtle (the inscription relates) is referred to in Verse 19 of Chapter 41 of the Book of Isaiah: "... *Ek sal in die woestyn gee die seder, die akasia en die mirt*..." ("... In the wilderness I shall put cedar trees, acacias, myrtles...")

Beside a small pond, bright with waterlilies in the sunshine of a summer's day and dotted with bulrushes, a neat plaque gives a biblical reference to water taken from Solomon's Song of Songs 4:15:

191

(Above) This monument stands adjacent to wheel-marks, set in concrete, of an ox-wagon which passed through Senekal in 1938 as part of the centenary celebrations of the Great Trek

(Above right) In the church garden, plaques provide Biblical references for many of the plants

"... U is 'n fontein van die tuine, 'n put met lewende water ...". ("... You are a fountain that makes the garden fertile, A well of living water ...")

And in the ponds are papyrus reeds from which paper was first made on which to record the word of God for generations to come.

There are many more: a charming and carefully chosen variety of shrubs, trees and beds of colourful roses and other flowers overlooked by two prominent memorial statues.

But, as interesting as this church itself is — for its architecture and its history — it is surely the unusual nature of these gardens and the uniqueness of its low encircling wall which are most significant, for this is no ordinary wall. Ornamented with fossilised trees in pieces of varying size, it provides a fascinating link with prehistory.

Some 250-million years ago (the geologists tell us) — that is about 100-million years before the evolution of man began — and when the present sandstone of the Free State was yet oozing mud, very little vegetation adorned the flat, swampy landscape. But in the area of Senekal odd forests of large trees broke the dreary emptiness of that steamy prehistoric landscape and it was from those trees, through countless aeons immured in the earth, that the fossils originated.

They link the present with an unbelievably distant past, signposts pointing reverently back to the Creation — "when God made heaven and earth": precious symbols gestated by nature herself, creations of the union of earth and time, evocative manifestations of an ancient, unwritten destiny which, millions of years later, led to the building of this modern place of worship close by.

Our Lady of the Assumption
Qwa Qwa

(Above)
The exterior of the Catholic church at Makwane, its plainness belying the richness of the art within

The name Qwa Qwa is probably as African in character as any appellation could be — as African in the staccato of its pronunciation as the raucous cry of a hadeda; and in its meaning laconically descriptive of the region of Qwa Qwa.

It is the home of the South Sotho, peoples who in the 1830s fled from marauding Zulu and took refuge in the broad valley between the Maluti Mountains and the rugged Drakensberg, whose peaks mark the southern edge of Africa's vast hinterland plateau. There the land falls away to lowlands which reach to the blue Indian Ocean.

Qwa Qwa lies in an area which, hundreds of millions of years ago, was covered by lakes and marshes that vanished in a volcanic era which laid basalt over much of the deposited silt. In the ensuing millennia erosion left hard patches protecting the compacted silt — in odd knolls and hillocks which, sculpted by wind and rain, are characteristic of the Lesotho landscape and the contiguous Orange Free State. The Sotho settlers named the place Qwa Qwa, meaning "White-white", after the colour of the surrounding sandstone mountains.

On the southern outskirts of the capital, Phuthadijaba, is the suburb of Makwane, situated beyond the end of the tarmac roads, past one-man workshops and open farmlands with their clusters of sheep and goats and patches of mealies — all set against the backdrop of the sandstone cliffs.

Approaching Makwane, one can see the red-brick Roman Catholic Church — Our Lady of the Assumption — its square tower stretching above an assortment of random buildings which are reached along a rutted track where habitation seems to peter out into grassy veld.

It is a plain and simple structure of fairly recent vintage, bare of external ornament, one of several places of worship scattered in the area.

One enters through a small porch beneath the tower, and at once the eye is drawn to the altar, set in an alcove of red brick that contrasts with the cream of the walls, and on it is an unusually beautiful tabernacle of copper and enamel. But, quickly, the eye moves again — upwards — captured by a magnificent carved figure of Christ crucified, clad in a simple cloak, suspended above the liturgical area. The fact that the figure here

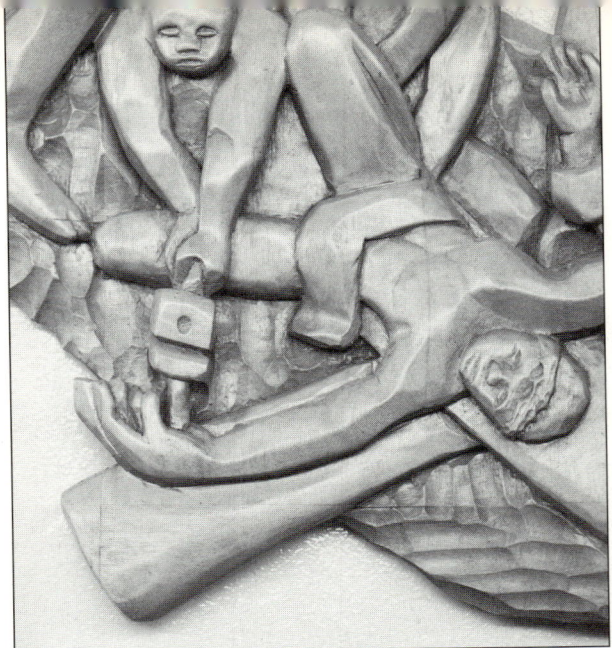

hangs freely in space emphasises the fact that Christ fills the universe and, unattached, is freely available to all. An angular bend to the outstretched arms gives the figure a dramatic vitality, which demonstrates His conquest of death and emphasises an abiding life which death can never take away.

This large figure, carved in honey-coloured wood, is fixed to an irregular symbolic Cross, the dark wood of which both holds the artistic composition together and gives emphasis to the body of Jesus it frames.

The sculpture was conceived and carved by Duke Ketye, a Xhosa artist who had his art training at Mariannhill near Durban. It was Ketye, too, who carved in similar light-hued wood the powerfully depicted Stations of the Cross on the side walls of the nave. The Stations themselves are linked by a painted frieze, showing the stony road to Calvary — represented by irregular rectangles and ovoid hoops that are reminiscent of the rocks of the rough roads of Africa — while the features of the carved figures, on rough bases, are also essentially African in character. The link with the region is made further manifest by the inclusion of typically local scenery in the background; the characteristic nipple-topped hillocks of Qwa Qwa bring the significance of the Crucifixion to this remote area.

When commissioned to execute this work Ketye asked whether he was expected to follow a traditional European style. In reply, he was told to illustrate the subject as he visualised it. Given such freedom of artistic expression, he created a unique and powerful interpretation of this universal theme for the people of the region, and, in doing so, added beauty that belies the external plainness of this out-of-the-way country church.

(Above, left and below) Duke Ketye's powerful carvings bring the Gospel to the people of Qwa Qwa

Nederduitse Gereformeerde Kerk
Kroonstad

*(Left)
Statue of Sarel Cilliers
by Coert Steynberg
in the grounds of
the church*

The early history of the northward spread of white settlers from the Cape in the nineteenth century repeatedly makes clear the need the Trekkers felt for places of worship wherever they halted and put down their roots.

The daily prayers said in the quiet privacy of their wagons and the more communal services of devotion held in the fresh air of the open veld while they travelled, required a more permanent location — a church — once the journey reached its end, and it was an accepted tenet that any Trekker settlement should give priority to the building of a church.

The settlement which developed into Kroonstad was no exception. The Trekkers there had settled over a wide area and farms were remote from one another. In 1854 Joseph Orpen was commissioned by the newly formed Free State *Volksraad* to find a site between the Renoster and Vals Rivers, agreeable to the settlers there, for the building of a church which would serve the scattered farmers and their families.

At the same time, Orpen "... was also to arrange the purchase or exchange of some land on both sides of the Valsch River at the drift on the main road, in order to lay out a township there..." He goes on to say that he gave the township the name Kroonstad "because there was already a Kroonspruit there." The stream had been named thus after a horse called Kroon which had died there.

The ground remained unused for several years, however, since, apparently unknown to the *Volksraad*, there was already a church serving the settlers in the area. It had been set up in 1852, shortly before Orpen's commission, by the

195

Voortrekker Sarel Cilliers, who had settled higher up on the Valsch River.

Plans were delayed by a number of factors and it was not until 1861 — the year that Kroonstad was officially inaugurated — that circumstances permitted the building of a new church. It was located in the centre of the little newly named town of Kroonstad, and its foundation stone was laid by the *Landdros*, Olaf John Truter, on 21 September. With construction completed in July 1862, a pulpit and communion table were awaited. Eventually the church was dedicated in January 1863, still without these important liturgical fittings. Two months later, according to the minutes of a meeting of the Church Council, "a sort of pulpit" was purchased for 30 shillings (R3)!

The building was a simple one, in the style of its time, with a dung floor and thatched roof, the stone for its walls brought to the building site voluntarily by members of the community. There were no pews or benches, however, and for some while members of the congregation were compelled to bring their own chairs to services, while for evening service each person also brought a candle.

This turned out to be the first of several Dutch Reformed Churches to serve Kroonstad's growing community.

In June 1866 the church council reported that the Dominee regarded the pulpit as being below standard, and a new one, together with a communion table, both of stinkwood and yellowwood, was purchased.

With the growth of the community and the congregation, it was not long before it became necessary to consider a larger church, and early in 1875 the foundations of the second Dutch Reformed Church were laid — for a building which, it was said, promised to be one of the most impressive buildings in Kroonstad.

That promise would seem to have been fulfilled. An English traveller in 1887 recorded that "The church at Kroonstad was the handsomest Dutch church I remember seeing in South Africa..."

It served the community for a number of years. Soon it became apparent, however, that yet again a larger church was required and funds were sought for its construction. By 1910, with 8 000 pounds in hand, it was possible to implement the scheme and W.H. Ford, an architect in Cape Town, was commissioned to design a church to accommodate 1 200 worshippers. The contract for its construction was given to H.J. van Jaarsveld, a builder who worked with his five brothers in the little town of Petrus Steyn.

The cornerstone was laid by Ds van der Lingen in December 1912. The dedication was taken from Chapter 2 of Saint Paul's Letter to the Ephesians: "... You are part of a building that has the apostles and prophets for its foundations, and Christ Jesus himself for its main cornerstone. As every structure is aligned on him, all grow into one holy temple in the Lord; and you too, in Him, are being

(Far left above)
The attractive architecture of the church creates strong patterns

(Left)
The symmetry of the organ pipes and the beauty of the finely proportioned and decorative pulpit create an attractive interior

built into a house where God lives, in the Spirit...."

This is the fine church, dedicated in 1914, which today graces the centre of Kroonstad, a town notable for a number of interesting and attractive places of worship.

Standing proudly in a large grassy square, this Dutch Reformed Moederkerk of local stone, with its tall honey-coloured tower and attractive Byzantine-style dome, impresses by its solid appearance and the strength of its proportions.

The gentle symmetry of its interior, free of harsh angular intrusions, creates an atmosphere of tranquillity. The forward area of the nave is dominated by the dome, while the light from the windows of the dome all around, diffused by the circular shape, is gently and subtly directed upon the main liturgical centre. The stuccoed ceiling is decorated in soft colours with rosettes around the central circular panel: an intrusion of baroque ornamentation unusual in a Dutch Reformed Church.

Above most of the nave a gallery stretches in an extended semi-circle, the panelling of its front consisting of decorated annealed dark metal panels.

The large windows of pale-tinted glass, high up, are edged with panels of decorated coloured glass, some with stylised floral patterns. The light is thus subtly toned, neither detracting from nor competing with the main illumination from the dome focused upon the central liturgical area.

The pews are of light-coloured wood, the forward semicircular rows filling the front section of the nave.

The impressiveness of the raised pulpit compels attention. It is wide, simply decorated and carved, with two plaques of pressed and darkened brass. Behind it is the organ with massive gilded pipes and above them a gilded inscription in a plastered arc across the front of the church: "*Heilig, Heilig, Heilig is die Heer.*"

Outside, on a corner of the grassy square, is a bold, bronze statue by Coert Steynberg of Sarel Cilliers, unveiled in 1950, while closer to the church building a smaller monument in white marble remembers the citizens of Kroonstad and the district who fell in the Anglo-Boer war.

This is an impressive church of which Kroonstad is justifiably proud; significant for the quality of its architecture and interesting for the history its embodies.

(Far left below)
The decorative dome illuminates the church

Photographic Notes

In 1855 in the preface to the second edition of his well-known classic, *The Seven Lamps of Architecture*, published not long after photography was "invented", John Ruskin, the famous nineteenth century art critic, wrote: "... the greatest service which can at present be rendered to architecture is the careful delineation of the details of the cathedrals... by means of photography." He went on: "... I would particularly desire to direct the attention of amateur photographers to this task; earnestly requesting them to bear in mind that while a photograph of landscape is merely an amusing toy, one of early architecture is a precious historical document..."

This belief in the value of photography as a means of recording architecture for posterity was echoed not long afterwards in South Africa when Mr Justice Cloete, opening a Fine Arts Exhibition in Cape Town in October 1866, spoke of the potential role of the camera in being able to record architectural details "in a few seconds by the collodion process..."

It is not only the grand cathedrals which should be photographically recorded for history, however. There are many other places of worship — more modest but, in their ways, no less beautiful and interesting — whose images similarly warrant places in the records of their times before falling victim to demolition, often prematurely, and before the future is forever denied a peep at its past.

To later generations, too young to have seen the reality of buildings and scenes which then no longer exist, the photographs themselves then become the reality.

As many will know, architectural photography, however ultimately rewarding, is one of the art's more exacting forms. There is the constant interference — in cities especially — of traffic and people, as well as of trees, power pylons and endless wires which cut across the view and which, somehow, seem to become more emphasised in a photograph than as the naked eye sees them in reality. But perhaps more difficult than that is the problem of fitting a large building squarely and visually upright into the camera's small viewfinder.

To retreat (if other obstacles do not intrude) is generally to produce a record of a building dwarfed by the foreground and too distant for its detail to be appreciated. The alternative is for the photographer to remain close — indeed, sometimes he has no option — but, of course, in such circumstances tilting the camera results in a distorted image of the building, its roof too small for its base, its vertical lines steeply converging.

In that preface Ruskin himself comes to grips with some of those problems but, in his zeal, urges the photographer not to be deterred but boldly to take the picture "... without regard to the resultant distortions of the vertical lines..." for, he suggests, such distortions can always be allowed for.

These difficulties — and more — have indeed cropped up in the compilation of this record. Furthermore, there are problems today which were not significant in Ruskin's time.

Traditionally churches are open for worship at all times and there should be no impediments to access. But that tradition is changing — indeed, has changed — and churches today, facing increasing robbery and vandalism, are not always readily open. To gain entry one often has to trace the whereabouts of the keys which seem to be held by a church official who frequently happens to be elsewhere just at that moment. There are, too, places of worship to which access is limited only to members of its congregation and where others are forbidden to enter for any reason whatsoever — and certainly not to take photographs.

This book is a modest attempt to demonstrate to South Africans something of the variety and richness of the church architecture around them and, briefly, to describe a little of the related historical and cultural connections. The illustrations are straightforward; the subjects need no artificial embellishments.

For larger format photographs, both colour and monochrome, a Hasselblad CM500 was used, with various lenses: viz. 80 mm Planar, 150 mm Sonnar, 250 mm Sonnar and 50 mm Distagon. For 35 mm pics Asahi Pentax cameras were used, with Pentax 17 mm Fish-eye lens, and Pentax 24 mm, 55 mm, 100 mm macro lenses as well as a Vivatar Series I 70-200 mm zoom: occasionally a Pentax (PC) Shift-lens. A Pentax Spotmeter and a Gossen Lunasix determined basic exposures.

With each format use was made of a spirit-level whenever feasible — as far as possible to eliminate the distortion which comes with tilting, either upwards or down. For architectural photography a spirit level is a most useful — if not essential — gadget, as also are a tripod and various filters.

For colour work — all transparencies — Agfachrome 100 and Agfachrome 50 were used, as well as Fujichrome 100. Some of the 35 mm pics were taken on Ektachrome 100HC. Black and white films included Ilford FP4 and HP5 as well as Agfapan APX100. The processing of the black and white film was done by the author himself, using Ilford ID11 or Rodinal developers. Printing — mostly on 23.3 x 25.4 cm Ilford Multigrade III RC paper — was done on a Chromega enlarger. Colour films were processed by Studio Nine in Pretoria and thanks go to Gert van Zyl and David Gritten and colleagues for the quality of their co-operation and service.

A frieze, by Barbara Greig, in the Catholic Cathedral in Kroonstad

Bibliography

Axelson, E.
South African Explorers,
World Classics: Oxford University Press, 1954.

Bailey, J.
The God-Kings and the Titans,
London, Hodder and Stoughton, 1965.

Bisschoff, E.
"The Mariamman Temple, Pretoria",
Unpubl. thesis, 1987.

Brabbs, D.
English Country Churches,
London, Weidenfeld and Nicolson, 1985.

Brown, W.E.
The Catholic Church in South Africa,
London, 1960.

Bull, M. and Denfield, J.
Secure the Shadow,
Cape Town, Terence McNally, 1970.

Bulpin, T.V.
Lost Trails of the Transvaal,
Cape Town, T.V.Bulpin, 1965.

Burchell, J.
Travels in the Interior of Southern Africa,
London, Longman, Hurst, Rees, 1822.

Coertzen, P.
The Huguenots of South Africa: 1688-1988,
Cape Town, Tafelberg, 1988.

Du Plessis, J.
*A History of Christian Missions
   in South Africa,*
London, Longmans, Green and Co, 1911.
Cape Town, Struik, 1965.

Davids, A.
The Mosques of Bo-Kaap,
Cape Town, SA Institute of Arabic and
   Islamic Research, 1980.

Davies, H. and Shepherd, R.H.W.
South African Missions: 1880-1950,
London, Thomas Nelson, 1954.

Dower, W.
*The Early Annals of Kokstad
   and Griqualand East,*
Durban, Killie Campbell Library, 1978.

Encyclopedia of World Religions,
London, Octopus Books Ltd, 1975.

New Columbia Encyclopedia,
Columbia University Press, 1975.

Standard Encyclopedia of Southern Africa,
London, Nasionale Boekhandel, 1972.

Foster, R.
Discover English Churches,
London, BBC, 1979.

Fisher, H.A.L.
A History of Europe,
London, E. Arnold and Co, 1936.

Fletcher, B.
*A History of Architecture on the
Comparative Method,*
London, B.T.Batsford Ltd., 1896 (rev).

Frazer, Sir James, OM,
The Golden Bough,
London, Macmillan, 1954 (rev).

Fransen, H.
Three Centuries of South African Art,
Johannesburg, A.D. Donker, 1982.

Garlake, P.
Great Zimbabwe,
London, Thames and Hudson, 1973.

Gordon-Brown, A.
Pictorial Art in South Africa — to 1875,
London, Chas J. Sawyer Ltd. 1952.

Gray, C. (Ed.)
Life of Robert Gray, Bishop of Cape Town,
London, Rivingtons, 1876.

Greene, G.
A Burnt-out Case,
London, Penguin Books, 1963.

Greig, D.
Herbert Baker in South Africa,
London, Purnell, 1970.

Grossert, J.
The Narasamy Temple,
Durban, S.A.Architectural Record, 1965.

Gutsche, T.
The Bishop's Lady,
Cape Town, Howard Timmins, 1970.

Hammond, P.
Liturgy and Architecture,
New York. Columbia U.P., 1961.

Harmsen, F.
The Way to Easter,
Pretoria, Joan Lotter, 1989.

Hedgecoe, J.
The Art of Colour Photography,
London, Mitchell Beazley, 1978.

Herod, F.G.
What Men Believe,
London, Methuen Educational, 1980.

Hinchliff, P.
The Church in South Africa,
London, SPCK, 1968.
The Church of England in South Africa,
London, SPCK, 1963.

Hollingworth, M.
Architecture of the 20th Century,
London, Bison Books, 1988.

Ive, A.
The Church of England in South Africa,
London, Church of England
   Information Office, 1966.

Keller, W.
The Bible as History,
London, Hodder and Stoughton, 1956.

Koorts, J.M.J.
Beginsels van Gereformeerde Kerkbou,
Bloemfontein, Sacum Beperk, 1974.

Langham-Carter, R.
Old St George's,
Cape Town, A.A. Balkema, 1977.

Lehmann, A.
Afroasiatische Christliche Kunst,
Friedrich Bahn Verlag, 1967.

Lewcock, R.
Early Nineteenth Century Architecture in South Africa,
Cape Town, Balkema, 1963.

Livingstone, D.
Livingstone's Missionary Travels in South Africa,
London, John Murray, 1857.

Marquard, M.
Letters from a Boer Parsonage,
Cape Town, Purnell, 1967.

Meer, F.
Portrait of Indian South Africans,
Durban, Avon House, 1969

Mikula, P. Kearney, B. and Harber, R.
Traditional Hindu Temples in South Africa,
Durban, Hindu Temple Publications, 1982.

Mitford, B.
Through the Zoolo Country,
Kegan Paul, Trench and Co. 1883.

Morris, D.
The Washing of the Spears,
London, Jonathan Cape, 1966.

Nolan, A.
God in South Africa,
Cape Town, David Philip (Pty), 1988.

Oberholster, J.J.
Historical Monuments of South Africa,
Cape Town, Rembrandt Foundation, 1972.

Ogilvie, G.
A Dictionary of South African Painters and Sculptors,
Johannesburg, Everard Read gallery, 1988.

Orbell, M.
The Natural World of the Maori,
David Bateman, 1985.

Parkes, J.
A History of the Jewish People,
London, Pelican Books, 1964.

Parrinder, G.
The World's Living Religions,
London, Pan Books, 1964.

Pearse, G.E.
Eighteenth Century Architecture in South Africa,
Cape Town, A.A. Balkema, 1968.

Pevsner, N.
An Outline of European Architecture,
London, Pelican Books, 1985 (rev).

Picton-Seymour, D.
Historic Buildings in South Africa,
Cape Town, Struikhof Publishers, 1989.

Randall, G.
The English Parish Church,
London, Batsford Press, 1988.

Raper, P.E.
Dictionary of Southern African Place Names,
Johannesburg, Lowry Publishers, 1987.

Reader's Digest,
Illustrated Guide to Southern Africa, 1980.

Ruskin, John.
The Seven Lamps of Architecture,
London, J.M. Dent and Co. 1849 (rev)

Schneider, H.
The Africans — an Ethnological Account,
Prentice-Hall: U.S.A, 1981.

Schoeman, K.
The Free State Mission,
Cape Town, Human and Rousseau, 1986.

Serfontein, D.
Kleurskrif vir Kroonstad,
Johannesburg, Perskor, 1990.

Shain, M.
Jewry and Cape Society,
Historical Publications Society, 1983.

Shimoni, G.
Jews and Zionism: the South African Experience,
Cape Town, Oxford University Press, 1980.

Spaarman, A.
Travels in the Cape: 1772-76,
VRS: Series II: Vol 6.
A Voyage to the Cape of Good Hope,
London, Robinson, 1785.
Cape Town, VRS, 1977.

Steele, R.
Destined to Win,
Johannesburg, Conquest Publishing, 1988.

Stewart, C.
Byzantine Legacy,
London, George Allen and Unwin Ltd, 1947.

Summerson, J.
Architecture in England,
London, Longmans Green, 1946.

Sundkler, B.G.M.
Bantu Prophets in South Africa,
Oxford University Press, 1964 (rev).
Zulu Zion and some Swazi Zionists,
Cape Town, Oxford University Press, 1976.

Thiel, J.J. and Helf, H.
Christliche Kunst in Afrika,
Berlin, Dietrich Reimer, 1984.

Thompson, G.
Travels and Adventures in Southern Africa,
London, Henry Colburn, 1827.
Cape Town, VRS, 1968.

Thunberg, Carl,
Travels at the Cape of Good Hope: 1772-1775,
VRS. : Series II - 17.

Trumpelmann, G.P.J.
Maleo en Sekoekoeni,
VRS, 1947.
Van Der Post L. and Taylor, J.
Testament to the Bushmen,
New York, Viking Press, 1984.
Walker, E.
A History of Southern Africa,
Longmans, 1968 (rev)
Wannenburg, A.
Forgotten Frontiersmen,
Cape Town, Howard Timmins, 1976.
Watkins, E.I.
Catholic Art and Culture,
London, Hollis and Carter, 1947.
Weyers, E.
Primitive Peoples Today,
London, Hamish Hamilton, 1959.
Willcox, A.R.
Southern Land,
Cape Town, Purnell and Sons, 1976.
Wilson, M. and Thompson, L.
A History of South Africa to 1870,
Oxford University Press, 1976.
Woodhouse, C. and Lee, D.N.
Art on the Rocks of Southern Africa,
Cape Town, Purnell and Sons, 1970.

A simple Cross in a private chapel at Kuruman

Index

Aaron, Bension 136
African man, primitive hunter-gatherer 6
African religions 27
Afrikaner, Jager 47
Albrecht, Christian 47
Albu, Rev Berthoud 66
Amboyna, Moslems from 63
Anglican Church, see Church of England;
 Church of the Province of South Africa
Anreith, Anton 36, 82
Architects
 Barac, Ivan 56
 Bisset 44
 Butterfield, William 61
 Das, Rajaram 123
 Ford, W.F. 196
 Gibb, James 77
 Harris, M.J. 157
 Kallenbach, Hermann 136
 Moerdijk, Gerard 141, 143
 O'Neill, Gorwyn 169
 Scott, Sir George Gilbert 58
 Simpson and La Gerche 138
 Till, J.H. and A.E. 185, 190
 Van Gemert, Jan 180
 Van Langenau, May 147
 Van Wijk, Jan 166
 Weichman and Read 77
Architecture, see entries for individual churches
 richness of styles in South Africa 112
Armstrong, Bishop 24
Asians 22

Backerius, Rev 34
Baker, Herbert 39
Bamberg, Bavaria 176
Bantu
 ancestor worship 14
 clashes with Bushmen 12
 dwellings 13
 early migration 13
 metal-working skills 12
 religious beliefs 13, 14
Baptists
 churches established 24
 Independent church 30
 promotion of Christianity 24
Barac, Ivan 56
Barends, Barend 103
Basuto War 1880-81 57
Bechuana Field Force memorial 57
Beckett, Rev Canon 181
Belvidere
 Holy Trinity Church 60-62
 rose window 62
 stained glass 62
Benedictine Order, Hlabisa 119
Berlin Mission

Bethany 187-9
Botshabelo 159-60
Bethany, OFS
 Berlin Mission Station 187-9
 land granted by Adam Kok 187
Bhaktivedanta, A.C. 122
Bibles
 collection of at Graaff-Reinet 45
 memorial to Afrikaans Bible 150
Bisset, architect 44
Blersch, Town Clerk, Stellenbosch 82
Bloemfontein
 Tweetoringkerk 174-7
 Anglican Bishop of 181
Blood River 94
Bonnievale, Myrtle Rigg Church 86-7
Borboreki, Zoltan 180
Botshabelo Lutheran Mission 159-61
Brand, President 176
Broom, Robert, discoveries at Sterkfontein 4
Bryant, Rev Dr Daniel 162
Buddha, Statue of 106, 107, 108
Buddhism 107, 108
Buffalo River, Natal 94
Builders
 Rowe, Marshall and Hill 190
 Rundle, Rowe and Marshall 184
 Van Jaarsveld, H.J. 196
Bulwer, Natal 109
Bulwer, Sir Henry 101
Bushmen, see San
Byzantine-style architecture
 Kroonstad 197
 Pretoria 142, 146

Calvinism, in Netherlands 21
Cambodia, ancient temples 6
Cape 17, 22, 34
Cape Town Castle 34
Carbineers, The Royal Natal 102
Carthage, attempts at colonising 3
Castle, see Cape Town Castle
Cave Church, Modderfontein 181
Champagne Castle, Drakensberg 115
Chanting, Hare Krishna ritual 124
China, relics from 12
Chinese
 early migrations to South Africa 25
 workers brought to South Africa 19
Christianity
 arrival in Africa 18
 arrival in South Africa 18
 first martyr in East Africa 16
 growth in modern Africa 29
 growth in South Africa 25
 in East Africa 18
 percentage of South African population 27
Church Building Act of 1818 (Britain) 58
Church of England
 bishopric established at Cape 23
 divisive problems 27
 early services at Cape 23
 numerical strength 27

Church of the Good Shepherd, Hlabisa 119-21
Church of the Province of Southern
 Africa 27, 39
Church of the Vow, Pietermaritzburg 94, 95
Church of the Vow, Louis Trichardt 95
Church of Saint Martin-in-the-Fields 77
Church silver
 Graaff-Reinet 45
 Bloemfontein 177
Cilliers, Sarel 196, 197
Coenen, J. 142
Coetzer, Willem 156
Colenso, Bishop
 appointment, Natal 18
 visit to Ladysmith 101
Collins, James 190
Colville, William 110
Council for Scientific and Industrial
 Research 166
Council of Policy
 establishment at Cape 20
 objection to baptism of Hottentots 71
 prayer of 20
Cradock
 Nederduitse Gereformeerde Kerk 75-7
 Sir John 75
Cry, the Beloved Country 1, 106

Dart, Professor Raymond 4
Da Silva, Father Gonzalo 19
Darwin, Charles 4
Davey, D. 110
Day of the Vow, history 94
De Klerk, F.W. 166
De Mist, Commissioner J.A. 21
De Roo, craftsman, Lydenburg 150
Dias, Bartolomeu 23
Dominican Order, missionaries
 in Mozambique 19
Doppers 27
Dower, Rev William 104
Dowie, Rev J.A. 30
Drakensberg, Natal, country church 115
Drakenstein, establishment of 22
Dravidian, temple architecture 25, 152
Durban
 Chapel at Old Fort 4
 Shree Poongavana Amman Temple 117-18
 Sri-Sri Radha-Radhanath Temple of
  Understanding 122-4
Dutch East India Company
 contact with Khoikhoi 8
 refreshment station at Cape 8, 20
Dutch Reformed Church
 early difficulties in recruiting ministers 24
 Bloemfontein (Tweetoringkerk) 174-7
 Cape Town (Groote Kerk) 34-6
 Cradock 75-7
 Graaff-Reinet 43-5
 Kroonstad 195-7
 Lydenburg 131, 148-50
 Middelburg (Transvaal) 154-6
 Pietermaritzburg 92-5

Potchefstroom 132-4
Pretoria East 141-3
Pretoria, Universiteitsoord 164-6
Senekal 190-92
Stellenbosch 82
Wakkerstroom 162
Winburg 184-6
Dutch Reformed Missionary Society 82
Duthie, Thomas Henry 61

Easter Island 11
Edwards, William 49
Egyptian pyramids 3
Ethiopia, early arrival of Judaism 18
Ethiopian Church in South Africa 30
Evans, Rev John 75

Faure, Sheikh Yusuf Kramat 63-5
Fauresmith 175
Fenwick, Pascoe 109
Fick, Antoon 149
Fire walking 118
Fossils, Senekal 192
Free Burgers, first settlers at Cape 21

Gabriel, Archangel, statue, Kroonstad 180
Ganesa 153
Gaudel, Father 47
Gcwenza, Bernard 119, 121
Genadendal, establishment of 26
  re-opening of 71
George, Brother 47
Germiston, Presbyterian Church 138, 140
Graham, Colonel John 57
Grahamstown
  Cathedral of St Michael and St George 57
  first Anglican Bishop 24
  first Methodists 18
  Methodist "Commem" church 52-4
Gibb, James 77
Gopirum 151
Govender, Yellapa 127
Graaff-Reinet, establishment of 22
  Dutch Reformed Church at 43-5
Grant and Downie 44
Gray, Robert 23
  consecrated St Andrew's church,
    Redbourne 80
  consecrated Cathedral, Grahamstown 57
Gray, Sophy 61
Great Synagogue, Johannesburg 135-7
Great Zimbabwe, *see* Zimbabwe
Greek Orthodox Church, Pretoria 146
Greig, Barbara 180
Griquas 103-105
  National Independent Church,
    Kokstad 103-5
Griqualand West Hebrew Association 66
Grossert, Professor Jack 121
Grutzner, Heinrich 159
Groves, Charles, ARCA 62
Groves, Mary 62

Hager, C.O. 155
Hamilton, co-worker of Moffat, Kuruman 49
Hatshepsut, Queen 3
Hare Krishna movement (ISKCON) 122
Healdtown 29
Hebrew Congregation, Johannesburg 136
  Old Witwatersrand Congregation 136
  United Congregation of Johannesburg 136
Heitsi Eibib 9
Hely-Hutchinson, Sir Walter 42
Hindu
  Dravidian architecture 25
  labourers from India 24
  temple ornamentation 118
Hindu temples
  Shree Poongavana Amman 117-18
  Subrahmanya temple, Tinley Manor 127-8
  Mariaman temple, Pretoria 151-3
Hlabisa 119
  Church of the Good Shepherd 119-21
Hogsback, Church of St Patrick on the Hill 85
Hottentot, *see* Khoikhoi
Houghton, Hobart 85
Huguenots 21
Hussars, memorials, Ladysmith 102

Independent Black Church 30
Indians
  early places of worship 25
  migrants to Natal 19, 24
Insandlwana 101
Interdenominational Chapel,
    Verwoerdburg 170-71
International Society for Krishna
    Consciousness (ISKCON) 122
Isaacs, Rev Harry 68
Isaiah 4

Janssens, Lieut-Gen. J.W. 21
Jesuits, missionaries in East Africa 19
Jews
  first at the Cape 24
  first congregation in South Africa 24
  first synagogue in South Africa 24
  first services on Witwatersrand 135
  Great Synagogue, Johannesburg 135-7
  Synagogue, Kimberley 66-8
  migrations to South Africa 135
Joubert, General P.J. 95
Judaism, early arrival in Africa 18
Jumallidin, "Chacha" 114

Kali 118
Kallenbach, Herman 136
Ketye, Duke 194
Khoikhoi
  arrival in southern Africa 8
  early European writings about 9
  religious beliefs 8, 9, 13
  skills 10
  social customs 8
Kimberley
  diamond industry 66
  Synagogue 66-8
Kinch, Father Edwin 121
Klip River, Natal 112
Knaap, Tertia 89
Kok, Adam 103
Kok, Jan 49
Kokstad 103-5
Krishna, Govindasany 151
Krishna 124
Kruger, Paul
  opens synagogue in Johannesburg 136
  role in Rustenburg break-away 27, 149
Kuruman
  "Eye" - perennial spring 49
  "fountain of Christianity in Africa" 51
  Moffat mission 49-51

Ladysmith, Natal
  All Saints Church 100-102
  Siege of 101
  Soofi Mosque 112-14
Lawley, Sir Arthur, KCMG 157
Lekganyane, Barnabas 145
Lekganyane, Edward 145
Lekganyane, Engennas 145
Lekganyane, Ignatius 145
Le Roux, Petrus Louis 162
Lesseyton, Cape 29
Lindley, Dr Daniel 184
Lion *Shul*, Johannesburg 157-8
Livingstone, David 51
Llandaff Oratory, Van Reenen 125-6
London Missionary Society
  Dower, Rev William 104
  early activities 26
  Kokstad 104
  Kuruman 49, 50
  Pella 47
Londt, Simon Pieter Christoffel 83
Lutherans, church in Cape Town 22
Lydenburg
  Nederduitse Gereformeerde Kerk 148-50
  origins of name 148
  retains links with Cape Synod 149

Makwane, Qwa Qwa
  Our Lady of the Assumption 193-4
Malaga, chapel 126
Malmesbury 22
Mamre, Moravian Mission 69-71
Marabastad 151
Mariaman Temple, Pretoria 151-3
Mariannhill Mission 96-9
Maritz, Gert 94
Markham, Rev Benjamin 110
Marks, Sammy 137
Marquard, Rev J.J.T 184
Mason, Professor Revil 6
Mathew, Llandaff 126
Mathew, Maynard 125
Mayan architecture 6
McCauley, Ray 167
Melvill, John 71

Methodists
    Commemoration church, Grahamstown 52-4
    contribution to education 28
    translation of Bible into Xhosa 28
Middelburg, Transvaal 155
    NGK 154-6
Millen, Hugh 50
Missionary Sisters of the Precious Blood 97
Missionaries
    first organised missionary work 25
    Grutzner, Heinrich 159
    Merensky, Alexander and Hans 159
    Moravian 26
"Missing link" 4
Mngoma, the Right Rev 99
Modderpoort, St Augustine's Anglican Mission 181-3
    cave church 181
Moffat, Mary 50, 51
Moffat, Robert 49
Mondi Paper Company Ltd 110
Monomotapa 19
Montefiore, Sir Moses 42
Moria 30, 144-5
Moshesh 181
Mozambique, Dominican missionaries 19
Murray, Rev Andrew
    laid cornerstone at Winburg 184
    minister at Bloemfontein 175
    minister at Graaff-Reinet 43
    recruited from Scotland 24
    visit to Lydenburg 149
Murray, Rev Charles 43
Murray, Rev John 132
Muruga, 153
Moslems
    hostility to Christianity in Africa 19
    labourers from India 24
    murder of Jesuit missionary 19
    placaat enabling Moslems to practise religion in private at Cape 63
    slaves from Malaya 22
    Soofi Mosque, Ladysmith 112-14
    workers from Amboyna 63
Mycenae, discovery 11

Naiker, Perumal, Tinley Manor Temple 127
Natalia, Republic of 94, 184
National Monuments Council 9
Nazareth 155
Nederduitsch Hervormde Kerk 19
Nederduitse Gereformeerde Kerk, see Dutch Reformed Church
Nederduitse Hervormde Kerk, Potchefstroom 132-4
Neethling, Rev 149
Newdigate, William 80
Nivard, Brother 97
Nuttall, Bishop 110

Ohrig, George 149
Ohrigstad 149

Old Fort, Durban 4
Onrus, Greek-style private church 88
Orpen, Joseph 195

Palframan 150
Paris Evangelical Society, in Orange Free State 181
Parker, J.H. 149
Paton, Alan 1, 106
Patriarch of Alexandria, Pope Nicalaos VI 147
Persia, ancient architecture 5
    relics from 12
Pevsner, Nikolaus 110
Pfanner, Father Franz 96, 97, 99
Philippolis 103
Phoenician circumnavigation of Africa 3, 7
Pietermaritzburg 94
    Church of the Vow 92-5
Piltdown Man 4
Plettenberg Bay
    Redbourne 79
    shipwrecked crew build chapel 23
Poen, schoolmaster in Lydenburg 149
Polynesia, monuments 6
Portuguese, early mapping of Africa 7
Potchefstroom 134
    independence from Cape Synod 149
    Nederduitsch Hervormde Kerk 132-4
Prabhupada, Swami 122
    effigy 124
Pretoria
    administrative capital of South Africa 141
    Greek Orthodox church 146
    Mariaman Hindu temple 151-3
    Nederduitse Gereformeerde Kerk 141-3
    Universiteitsoord 164
Pretorius, Marthinus Wessels 132
Pulver, Rev Isaac, Rabbi 40
Punt (East Africa) 3
Pyramids, Egypt 3, 6

Queenstown, Cape 55
    Roman Catholic Cathedral of Christ the King 55-6
    St Michael's Anglican Church 55
Qwalana, Rosina 71
Qwa Qwa 193
    Our Lady of the Assumption, Makwane 193-4

Randburg 167
Rand Club 135
Redbourne, Yellowwood church at 79-80
Religion, in early Africa 8
    of Khoikhoi 13
    of San 13
    twentieth century in Africa 14
Retief, Pieter 94
Rhema Church, Randburg 167-9
Rhenish church, Stellenbosch 81-3
Rhenish Mission, short-lived occupation of Pella 47
Rhenish Missionary Society 81

Rigg, Christopher 86, 87
Rigg, Mary Myrtle, memorial church at Bonnievale 86-7
Roman Catholics
    ban on at Cape 21, 22
    Bishop's residence permitted 28
    contribution to education 28
    early chapel at Plettenberg Bay 23
    first Mass in South Africa, 1497 23
    first place of Christian worship in South Africa 23
    first resident priests, 1804 22
    practice of faith prohibited at Cape 28
    strength of in South Africa 27
    visit of priests to Cape 22
Rustenburg, formation of Gereformeerde Kerk 27, 149

Saint, see St
San (Bushmen)
    appearance and character 10
    art 10, 11
    early settlements 9, 10
    religion 13
Sandburg, Carl 80
Santa Sophia, Istanbul 137, 147
Schliemann, Heinrich 5
Schmidt, Georg 26, 71
Selhorst, Sister Pientia, C.P.S.
    art work at Mackay's Nek 72
    art work at Mariannhill 99
    art work at Queenstown 56
Senekal, Nederduitse Gereformeerde Kerk 190-92
Settlers, 1820 24
Settlers' Window, "Commem" church, Grahamstown 53
Servite (Roman Catholic) Order 121
Shree Poongavana Amman Temple, Durban 117-18
Sick Comforter, responsibilities at Cape 20
Silk Road 16, 19
Simon, Father 47
Simpson and La Gerche 138
Skotnes, Cecil, 178
Slaves, importation of 22
Smith, Roland 115
Snake River, Wakkerstroom 162
Society of Saint Augustine 181
Soofi Mosque, Ladysmith 112-14
South African Christian Missionary Society 81
Sri Ramakrishna, quotation 3
St Andrew's Presbyterian Church, Germiston 138
St Augustine 181
St George's Cathedral, Cape Town 37-9
St Luke's Chapel, Onrus 88-9
St Michael's Cathedral, Grahamstown 57-9
St Michael's Church, Queenstown 55
St Pancras, London 37
St Patrick Cathedral, Kroonstad 178-80
St Patrick on the Hill, Hogsback 84-85
St Peter-in-Chains, Durban 4

Stations of the Cross
    Kroonstad 178
    Makwane, Qwa Qwa 194
    Queenstown 56
Stellenbosch
    establishment of 22
    Turf Club, donates ground to church 81
Sterkfontein 4
Steytler, Maxie 89
Steyn, M.T. 184
Steynberg, Coert 134
    statue of Sarel Cilliers, Kroonstad 197
Stonehenge 5
Subrahmanya temple, Tinley Manor 127-9
Sudan, Khoikhoi contact with 8
Sumerians, ziggurats 5, 11
Sumner, Maud 180
Swart, C.R. 166
Synagogues
    Cape Town, old and new 40
    Johannesburg 157-8
    Kimberley 66-8

Tamil, Temple, Pretoria 151
    ornamentation 117
Taung, discovery of fossilised skull 4
Taylor, Rev John 76
Terry, W.J. 182
Theron, Leo 89
Till, John Henry and A.E. 186
Tinley Manor, Natal, Shiva temple 127-9
Torah pointer, diamond-tipped, Kimberley 68
Trappist Mission, Mariannhill 96
Trekkers, wish for independence 27
Truter, Olaf John 196
Tsetse-fly 12
Tsui-Goab 9
Tulbagh, Cape 22
Tulsa, USA 167
Tweetoringkerk, Bloemfontein 174-7
Twells, Dr Edward 181

Ulufafa River, Natal 106
Umzimkulu River, Natal 106
United Congregational Church, Kuruman 51

Van Arckel, Johan 22
Van der Hoff, Rev Dirk 133
Van der Linger, Ds 196
Van der Velden, Ds Dirk 184
Van Gogh, C.V. 177
Van Loon, Louis 107
Van Reenen, Natal, site of Llandaff
        Oratory 125
Van Rensburg, Jack 89
Van Riebeeck, Jan 20
    conversion of Hottentot, Eva 26
Van Vuuren, 151
Vedic culture, renaissance 122
VOC, *see* Dutch East India Company

Wakkerstroom, Transvaal 30, 162
    churches 162-3
    Dutch Reformed Church 162, 163
Warden, Major 175
Wasbank, Natal 94
Webb, Bishop 59
Weichman and Read 77
Wesleyans, missionaries in eastern Cape 26
    establish seminary for blacks 29
    separatist church 21
Whitefriars Studio, England 180
Williams, Rt Rev Frederick 59
Winburg 175
    Dutch Reformed Church 184-6
"Witkerk", Middelburg, Transvaal 154-6
Wocke, R. 176
Wolf, Brother 48
Wooden churches
    in South Africa 79
    oldest in world 79
    yellowwood church at Bulwer 109-11
    yellowwood church at Redbourne 79-80
Wuras 187

Xhosa, Bible translated 28
Xulu, Ruben 119, 121

Yellowwood Chapel of the Holy Trinity,
        Bulwer, Natal 109-11
Yellowwood Church of St Andrew,
        Redbourne 79-80
Yemen, migrants to Africa from 12
Yusuf, Sheikh, Kramat at Faure, Cape 63-5

Zandvliet 65
Zimbabwe, buildings 7, 12
Zionist Christian Church
    headquarters at Moria 30, 144
    divisions 30, 144
Zionist churches 30, 144

Founders' cemetery, Bethany